Praying Our Experiences

An
Invitation
to Open
Our Lives
to God

D1040606

JOSEPH F. SCHMIDT, FSC

Foreword by
BENEDICT J. GROESCHEL, CFR

Praying Our Experiences

*An
Invitation
to Open
Our Lives
to God*

JOSEPH F. SCHMIDT, FSC

the WORD among us® Press

The Word Among Us Press,
7115 Guilford Drive, Suite 100
Frederick, Maryland 21704
wau.org

18 17 16 15 14   7 8 9 10 11
ISBN: 978-1-59325-116-1
eISBN: 978-1-59325-419-3
Cover design by Laura Steur-Alvarez

Library of Congress Cataloging-in-Publication Data
Schmidt, Joseph F.
Praying our experiences : an invitation to open our lives to God / Joseph F.
Schmidt. -- [Updated & expanded ed.].
p. cm.
ISBN 978-1-59325-116-1 (alk. paper)
1. Prayer. I. Title.
BV215.S355 2008
248.3'2--dc22

2007051881

Other books by Joseph F. Schmidt, FSC
Praying with Thérèse of Lisieux
Everything Is Grace: The Life and Way of Thérèse of Lisieux
Walking the Little Way of Thérèse of Lisieux

Contents

FOREWORD

Real prayer is a total experience, bringing together all the strands of our lives. Brother Joseph Schmidt thoughtfully and sensitively describes many of these different strands, ranging from God's word coming to us in the Scriptures to our own willingness to grow beyond our selfishness to maturity. By focusing on praying our experiences, he wisely interprets our many inner personal experiences as prayer, or at least as the stuff from which serious prayer is made.

This book is intended, on the one hand, for those who are just beginning to take the personal experience of prayer seriously. And, on the other hand, it is intended for those already traveling on the road of prayer and who now need to reexamine their prayer life and its individual components with the goal of growing still more in prayer. Of course, all true prayer must be guided and inspired by the Holy Spirit, but in prayer and in many other things, God helps those who help themselves.

This book explores the road of "telling our story to God," suggesting that we pray with our life experiences in mind. This way of prayer is best illustrated by the *Confessions* of St. Augustine and the autobiographies of the two great Carmelite Church doctors, Teresa of Ávila and Thérèse of Lisieux.

Praying Our Experiences: An Invitation to Open Our Lives to God is a newly revised and expanded version of a book that has been in print for over a quarter of a century, through three editions and 100,000 copies. It has been used in classrooms, retreat centers, spiritual direction institutes, twelve-step programs, evangelization sessions, and formation and catechetical classes. When this book originally appeared, many different types of prayer were being written about and practiced. They ranged from charismatic prayer to centering prayer. The strength and usefulness of this book are due to its concentrated focus on the simple gospel truth that our need for prayer comes from the heart—that is, from the center of the person's being—and is founded in our life experiences. The heart, of course, is a symbol of the center of all our desires, hopes, needs, intelligent ideas, and character strengths. They all come together in the light of grace.

Whatever purifies our heart and strengthens its influence in the activities of life is a help to real prayer. This fact makes the serious desire to live and pray from the experiences that touch our heart all the more essential for a life of real prayer. As we become genuinely more prayerful, prayer will direct our lives, and we will not have to struggle consciously to lift our hearts to God. Our heart will "surge" to God, as St. Thérèse assures us, and will carry the deepest sentiments of our lived experiences. St. Paul expresses this so well: "It is no longer I who live, but it is Christ who lives in me" (Galatians 2:20). Even in times of temptation, trial, failure, or spiritual aridity, God will be there in prayer, and the Son of God will shepherd us.

Following the teaching of St. John Baptist de La Salle, founder of the Brothers of the Christian Schools, the congregation to which he belongs, the author includes an important consideration about the relationship between prayer and the ministry of good works. This discussion of the spirituality of ministry is very worthwhile. While we have layers of motivation in doing good, ranging from self-centeredness to altruism, it would be unwise to try to limit our activities to those that seem purely altruistic. That is not the road of spiritual development and growth. We would do well to follow the advice of Thérèse and Teresa of Ávila, who suggest that self-knowledge that arises as we actually do good works is integral to prayer. Helpful, too, is the pointed directive of the Christian Brothers' founder to "examine before God how you are acting in your ministry and whether you are failing in any of your responsibilities. Come to know yourself just as you are . . . so that when Jesus Christ comes to judge you, you may be able to face His judgment without being afraid."

In the not very distant past, when large numbers of people became interested in contemplative prayer, apostolic activity was seen by some almost as a necessary evil and a distraction. Then we moved into a time of extreme activity, when prayer was thought to be a form of self-indulgence and self-preoccupation. Praying our experiences helps us to achieve a necessary balance and integration.

It is certainly hoped that we will get the balance right, as a new interest in both prayer and good works is observable in the John Paul II generation, that group of young adults who are among those who will continue to revitalize the church. With solid religious education, especially in the area of prayer as personal relationship with God founded in their lived experiences, they will find a way to blend activity with prayer. Whether they are seriously practicing Catholic laity or, in growing numbers, sincere and integrated candidates for religious life or the priesthood, all agree that work and prayer go together. Working with many young Catholics at the present time, I realize that the very points the author brings out in focusing on praying our experiences are well attuned to the spiritual needs of the young at this time.

No matter how old we are or where we find ourselves—whether new on the religious scene or a veteran of the battles of recent decades—the insights in this book will be helpful in our life of prayer.

Benedict J. Groeschel, CFR

PREFACE

There are many ways to pray. There may, perhaps, be as many ways of prayer as there are people seeking to find and respond to God, who is first and always seeking us. Some people find their response to God in spontaneous prayers of blessing and praise, prayers of petition, intercession, and thanksgiving; some, as they recite devotional prayers found in a favorite prayer book. Others pray as they share prayer in groups or participate in the celebration of the liturgy. Still others pray best by reciting traditional prayers such as the rosary or by reflecting on the words of Scripture or by simply being present to God in receptivity and listening. Some may not pray in any particular "way" at all.

This book will focus on one way of individual private prayer that is traditional and fundamental but at the same time is also informal, personal, intuitive, and often spontaneous. It is available to everyone; we do not need a book to engage in this kind of prayer; and it is as unique as each one of us. In fact, we may already be praying this way without even realizing it, but we may need to more consciously develop this form of prayer. We might call this kind of prayer "praying our experiences."

Many of us have already sensed that sincere reflection on the ordinary experiences of our lives has a prayer value. As we look over the times that have been occasions of prayer and spiritual growth for us, we realize that some of these times, perhaps even the majority, have occurred when we took stock of ourselves and got in touch with the significance of an event in our life. It might have been when we reflected on a brief phone call from a friend at a time of grief, when we endured an illness, or when we wondered about the meaning of years of discouragement and frustration. It might have been when we thoughtfully reconsidered a momentary argument, a period of personal tension and confusion, or a word of support and encouragement. As we pondered and reminisced, we might not have thought that we were praying; but in retrospect, we find that as we reflected on our experiences and grappled with their truth and meaning all the elements of prayer were present: we felt the sinfulness of being ego-centered; we felt the graciousness of God's work in us; we felt, simply, the closeness of the Lord and the call to a deeper authenticity in our life. We have been praying our experiences.

When we pray our experiences, we reflect on and consider more than simply the external characteristics of an event or even our sensory awarenesses of an occurrence. By "experiences" we include not just *what* we have perceived—the splendors of nature, the news of a war, a passage in a novel, the imagery of a poem, a scene in a movie, the beauty of music, the joys of a relationship, the receipt of an award, the pain of an injury—but also *who* we are now as the person who has been affected by this awareness. In praying our experiences, therefore, we also intend to include all of the awarenesses and feelings, thoughts, memories, and desires that are generated by our experiences.

Praying our experiences means responding to our experiences in a spirit of honest engagement, searching for the truth of who we are in those experiences. We seek to open ourselves to the meaning of our experiences to receive God's love and providence.

This way of prayer may sometimes take the form of speaking to the Lord about our experiences in a simple, direct, and very personal way. Prayer formulas may not always appropriately or adequately express the heartfelt feelings of joy or distress that we wish to share with the Lord; nor may a particular formal way of prayer help us to be in touch with the totally unique and private happenings of our life experiences.

When we pray our experiences, then, we use experiences as the content of our prayer so that we can get in touch with who we are as the person who has had these experiences, who has lived that part of our story, and then offer that "who" to God through honest reflection on the experiences. Praying our experiences thus involves more than daydreaming, more than reminiscing, more than planning, more than pouting over the past. That is not to say that daydreaming or pouting couldn't themselves be an experience that we make the content of a prayer offering—all of our experiences, joyful and distressful, can be the content of our prayer.

In praying our experiences, we gather the fragments of our life to become aware of who we are, not to perform some psychological exercise of self-understanding, or to engage in some legalistic activity of self-evaluation, or to enter some moral or ethical process of fixing our life and becoming more functional. All of these things may happen, but our prayer is founded on the willingness and simplicity of being present to God in the unfolding of our story in honesty.

Praying our experiences is a way of prayer that is valid and traditional, and for some it is a preliminary departure point in the journey of prayerfulness, constantly recurring because it is such a personal and intuitive way of praying. Nevertheless, it is sometimes not recommended or consciously attempted as a way of prayer, perhaps because of the fear that it could degenerate into self-centeredness. Yet, when it is approached with sincerity, reflection on our experiences can ultimately lead to a depth of self-knowledge that actually purges self-centeredness and has the potential to bring us to greater intimacy with God.

Ironically, praying one's experiences is exceedingly common among people who—not understanding it to be prayer—condemn themselves for not praying.

The following pages will explore the implications of sincere reflection on our experiences as a way of prayer.

1. Established in Tradition

Life Experiences as the Focus of Prayer

When we are private and alone, we each pray in our own way. As we open our hearts to God, our prayer arises out of our personal joys and sorrows, our unique desires and longings. The general pattern that our prayer takes, however, is often similar to one or more of the three ways that people over the centuries have ordinarily prayed. The Christian spiritual tradition has called these three ways of prayer reflective prayer or meditation, affective prayer, and contemplative prayer.

Reflective prayer or meditation is a mind-centered approach to prayer, employing discursive thought and often including the use of the imagination to focus on an incident of the Scriptures or the lives of the saints. In this prayer, we might reflect in a meditative way on a situation in the life of Jesus, such as his passion and death, applying to our life a challenge from the example of Jesus' life. Or we may think through the significance of a saying of Jesus, or ponder the meaning that a parable offers to our own life. Or, in our imagination, we may participate in a scriptural scene, deriving inspiration and meaning from the interaction with the figures in the scene.

Affective prayer focuses more directly on our willingness to share our feelings with God, to talk to Jesus about our life, our anxieties, and our desires. We might express our affections in words from Scripture: "Lord, to whom can we go? You have the words of eternal life" (John 6:68) or "Lord, be my shepherd; be my joy" (see Psalm 23). We might simply recite slowly the Our Father or Hail Mary. We might pray the rosary or repeat a short aspiration: "Lord, I love you," "My Lord and my God," or just repeat slowly a form of the Jesus prayer, "Lord Jesus, Son of the living God, be merciful to me, a sinner." Or we might simply say the name of Jesus. In each case, we let our personal expression of faith carry the longings and sentiments of our heart.

Contemplative prayer is the name given to the form of prayer that doesn't primarily focus on reflecting on the Scriptures or the life of a saint, or even focus primarily on expressing our feelings and sentiments toward God. Rather, in contemplative prayer, we simply rest in the presence of God in loving, listening awareness. We are available and open to the reality of union with God and rejoice in that union.

These three ways of praying, of course, do not tell the whole story of prayer, since the Holy Spirit prays as the Spirit wills. Each of us prays in our own way; and, in a sense, it is not really "our" prayer at all, since the Spirit prays within us—within our personal gifts and limitations—in ways that we do not even know (see Romans 8:26-27).

Nor, of course, are these ways of prayer mutually exclusive. We do not pray solely one way to the exclusion of other ways. Our starting point for personal, private prayer can be where we are most comfortable. We do well to begin our prayer where, at the moment, we are drawn to begin. But even when we have a preference and an intention to pray in a specific way, and even if we do indeed begin to pray in the way we prefer, we may sometimes find our prayer changing. Our prayer certainly changes over the years, but even in the course of a single period of personal prayer, we will often find our prayer moving back and forth across the continuum of reflective prayer, affective prayer, and contemplative prayer.

Understanding the traditional three ways of prayer and the rhythm among them, we can place the notion of "praying our experiences" within this tradition. When we speak of "praying our experiences," we are referring to focusing on our own life experiences as the content, the subject matter, of our time of personal prayer. Since we are drawn to this kind of prayer by our lingering memories and continuing feelings, praying our experiences often begins in a reflective way. That is, we begin to think about or meditate on our life or a particular experience of our life. Thus, instead of focusing our considerations and our imagination on an incident in the Scriptures or a situation in the life of Jesus, we begin our prayer by recalling a situation in our own life. The situation might sometimes be a joyful one; it might sometimes be a painful one.

We might, for example, pray the experience of an argument that turned hurtful and bitter that we had the previous week with a colleague. Now, with several days' distance from that experience, our temper has calmed and our mind cleared, and we are willing to bring the experience before the Lord. We do not foster self-condemnation or the condemnation of anyone else. We do not promote an attitude of trying to improve ourselves or fix ourselves up; nor do we enter our prayer trying to improve or fix up our colleague. We do not do a moral inventory. But through our willingness to be honest as we recall the incident, we simply open ourselves to welcome the truth of the experience. We are willing to let the Lord fix us and improve us in the Lord's own time.

As we reflect on the details of the argument, we may remember that we did manage to control ourselves to some extent on the outside. But we recall that our thoughts and speech were sarcastic and demeaning toward our colleague; and from the awareness of our defensiveness and the disturbance of our lingering feelings, we know that on the inside, we had made our colleague an enemy, if just for the time of the argument. We had nurtured, if not actually expressed, excessive feelings of disappointment, anger, and hostility. We had, perhaps, for a time, harbored feelings of bitterness and retaliation. And in retrospect, we know that we had entered an egotistic, self-centered, defensive place, which was not our best self and to which we had not been called by the Holy Spirit.

In praying such an experience, we take time to explore the feelings and thoughts that led up to the argument, our unmet needs and desires that contributed to our hostility. We reflect on our expectations of ourselves and of our colleague that we brought to the argument and that allowed us to be drawn into that hurtful state. We might ponder what it was that really aroused our anger, and we might consider what we were really defending in our hostility. We might consider also how our self-image might have furthered the argument. In short, we meditate on ourselves and what was actually happening within us that made it necessary for us to contribute our share of violence to that hurtful argument.

The argument might have been based on our perception that something needed to be changed, but in praying our experiences we do not try to rationalize or justify ourselves. We need to recall that Jesus has told us how to deal with our enemy, and how to address any situation that requires changing. We are called to be reconciled with our enemy, to love our enemy (Matthew 5:44). And we are called to address evil and to contribute to any change, not by violence, but in a spirit of inner freedom, compassion, and creativity. None of that loving spirit was present in the hurtful argument.

In praying our experiences, we try to be as honest as we can, focusing on what was going on in us that contributed to this unholy situation. In this prayer, we are willing to bear the pain of seeing ourselves as imperfect. We are also willing to hold onto the hope that we are called to eventually do something forgiving, loving, creative, and healing within ourselves and in relationship to our colleague in response to that hurtful argument.

As our reflective prayer on our painful experience continues, we may find our prayer moving back and forth across the continuum of the three ways of prayer. From meditating on our contribution to the hurt of the experience and gaining some insight into the truth of ourselves, our prayer might shift to a more affective prayer of directly speaking to the Lord, asking for further clarity, honesty, forgiveness, and reconciliation. Then we may be able to come with more peace into the embrace of God, who has already forgiven us and our enemy. Our prayer now moves into the contemplative stance of resting in a loving God, willing to surrender to the reality of who we are in God's embrace.

In praying our experiences, we reflect on the story of our life in relation to God, and in so doing, we place our story into God's story. That is, by honestly searching our motives and exploring what was going on inside us, we enfold our experiences into the truth of the gospel—the truth that is already within us as the Spirit of Truth, abiding in us and constantly calling us to be our true, best self.

It is, of course, not just difficult situations that can form the content of praying our experiences. We can pray our joys as well, the consoling experiences that tell us of the power of the Spirit in us and that invite us to delight in God's gifts in our life. Then we are challenged to become more conscious of God's goodness, not only in the experiences of consolation, but in all the experiences of our life.

Using our own experiences as the content, the subject matter of our prayer puts us in the company of the holy men and women of the Scriptures, the prophets, and indeed Mary and Jesus, who prayed their experiences as they searched for a deeper understanding of the mystery of Divine love.

We notice, for example, that the main focus of Job's prayer was, of course, the meaning of his own suffering. He did not deny or ignore his plight or keep it apart from his prayer by saying a prescribed prayer of the community that might have been irrelevant to his confusion and pain. Rather, he pondered his predicament and struggled with the truth that might be hidden in his suffering.

Mary's efforts to understand the meaning of the angel's words at the annunciation are also an example of prayer surging from within the heart of lived experience.

Mary may have been at prayer, meditating on the psalms or conversing with the Lord as she went about tidying up the house. But she was interrupted in her prayer by a sudden awareness, which Luke describes as the message of an angel: "Rejoice, O highly favored daughter. The Lord is with you. Blessed are you among women" (see Luke 1:28-38).

Mary was troubled and wondered what the greeting meant. "Do not be afraid, Mary," the angel said, "for you have found favor with God. And now, you will conceive in your womb and bear a son, and you will name him Jesus."

Now Mary's disturbance was deep indeed. Feelings of anxiety were aroused in her. How, she wondered, could this be? Her awareness of God's presence and the inkling of what was being asked of her challenged deep areas of her self-identity. Who was she, to be so favored by God, to be asked to involve herself in such a way in the work of salvation?

"I do not know man." Now thoughts of her family, of her decision to marry Joseph, feelings of confusion and fear all must have surged up in Mary. "What does the Lord want? What am I called to do? How can this be possible?" But Mary was open to her Lord; she wanted to hear the truth; she desired so much to accept the will of her God. What could all this mean?

Perhaps Mary's reflections and struggle lasted for a few minutes or a few hours; perhaps they continued for a few days or many weeks. Luke telescopes the scene into a continuing dialogue and says that the angel answered Mary, "The Holy Spirit will come upon you, and the power of the Most High will overshadow you. . . . Nothing will be impossible with God."

And now Mary knew that she was being called to be possessed by the power of God in her life. She was being asked to give up the subtle resistance raised by her self-image, her personal plans, her previous decisions, her own agenda in life.

She prayed this experience with all its memories and all its feelings of confusion and fear, of joy and surrender. She did not dismiss the angel's announcement as an intrusion into her daily prayer schedule. Rather, struggling to come to the truth of her life in the presence of God, her conversing with the angel became her prayer.

Luke's story of the annunciation is the story of Christian prayer. Mary opened her heart to her God by hearing and responding to God's call. Her prayer was to search for truth, for meaning in her life; and through the overshadowing of the Spirit of Truth, she was the first to receive him who would call himself the Truth. To receive this Truth, Mary needed to accept a new self-identity and open herself to a completely unexpected future.

This very intuitive way of praying—used by Job and Mary and other holy men and women in the Scriptures, including Jesus himself, when, for example, he prayed in his agony in the garden—has also been the way ordinary Christians throughout the centuries have prayed, reflecting on their lived experiences, searching for Divine providence in the unfolding of their lives. And it can be our way of praying, as well.

We may surely use the prayers of Job or Mary—or of anyone else, for that matter—as the basis of our own prayer, but we should be careful not to pray *their* life experiences instead of praying our own. The truth that Job came to understand in

24

his experiences and that Mary understood in hers can be helpful truths for understanding our experiences, but they can never take the place of our own unique prayer to God. After all, God has already heard the prayer flowing from Job's and Mary's experiences, but God has not yet heard the prayer flowing from our experiences.

2. Reflecting on Our Life

To Know Ourselves as God Knows Us

Few of us tend to think that we pray well, and the reason may be that we have too many misconceptions about what constitutes "good" prayer. For instance, we tend to think of prayer as something that originates with us and is always conscious to us, rather than as something motivated by God; we think that prayer has to have a lofty content or that the words need to come from a book. We assume that our prayer time has to be focused, and that we've failed at praying if our mind wanders. And yet, if we allow the Holy Spirit within us to "pray as the Spirit wills," we may find that our prayer occurs also when we let go of these self-imposed constraints and allow the experiences of our life—as we reflect on them in honesty—to become the content of our prayer. By allowing God to direct our prayer in this way, we allow God to speak to us by showing us ourselves as only God knows and loves us. This is what happened to Larry and Sue.

"I couldn't believe what Frank said to me," Larry told the priest in the confessional. "We've been drinking buddies for twenty years, and he usually jokes all the time. Then, out of the blue, he had to get serious and say, 'Hey, pal, that's not right.' Maybe it was the way he said it, or maybe it was just the way I heard it, but I was stunned."

"And then what?" the priest asked.

"Well, I just thought about it; that was all. I figured I needed to do something, and that's why I came to confession."

What Larry had begun to think about were his business trips, and especially the drinking and the one-night stands that lately went with them. He had rationalized to himself that everyone drank and fooled around. And besides, his wife and children didn't know, and so no real harm was being done. But his friend's out-of-the-blue comment had jolted him to reconsider.

Then one afternoon as Larry was routinely driving along an open highway on his way to meet a client, his friend Frank's remark came back to him. He felt some inner resistance at first, but he turned off the car radio and began to think. Instead of arguing with himself or trying to justify himself, he let the entire matter of the business trips, the drinking, and the sexual encounters surface in his awareness. He remembered the pattern of his actions during those times; he recalled the anticipation, the dissatisfaction, the guilt, the personal distress.

Even as his memory worked, he noticed feelings of anxiety, fear, and embarrassment welling up in him. He became aware of his desire to blame circumstances and his wife for what he was beginning to see as his own personal weakness. He realized that he wanted to forget the whole thing, to decide firmly to start over and let the past be past. He began to recite a prayer he had learned as a child. Then he realized that he was really trying to get rid of the pain that was surging up in him, as the reality of these "incidents," as he called them, became more and more clear.

The memory and feelings associated with the drinking and the one-night stands were painful, agonizingly painful. And he hated the pain. But he also knew that there was a truth to be found in the memory and in the pain. He had had a hint of the importance of his taking that truth seriously when he felt the power of his friend's simple statement: "Hey, pal, that's not right."

Now, as he drove silently along an empty stretch of highway, Larry let the pain come on him. He simply waited. He resisted turning on the radio or daydreaming. He just waited in the fear and pain. There was nothing dramatic, but gradually he felt a kind of clarity, and then all the questions started to come: "What is really going on that causes so much drinking? What are you really looking for in these one-night stands? Who are you becoming by doing these things? Where is God in these experiences?" And then Larry knew that his friend's remark had really been God's way of giving him a stiff kick. That's when he decided to get some help.

A month or so later, Larry told his friend that he had done some thinking and that he had gone to confession and was seeing a counselor.

Larry never considered his reflections during that routine automobile drive as prayer. Prayer, for him, was something you did in church, or with formulas you had memorized as a child, or with readings out of a prayer book or the New Testament. And in any case, when you prayed, you had something pious to say to God. None of this applied to that time of thinking as he drove silently, reflectively, seeking to find some truth and peace in his experience.

Sue's story of a time of prayer is similar to Larry's. Each day after she got Eddie off to school, Sue had the practice of spending fifteen minutes sitting in the living room, reading psalms from her Bible. She read consecutively and slowly. On any given day, she would get through only one psalm or part of one. She especially liked the psalms of praise, which she used as the basis for her own prayers of praise to God for all the wonderful things God had done for the chosen people.

On one such occasion, she suddenly realized that Eddie had left his lunch on the floor by the door. She knew she would have to drop it off at school later in the morning. That made her think of Eddie's spontaneous way of doing things, which sometimes got him into trouble (he had forgotten his lunch after putting it down to give her a big hug and kiss), and then she thought of how he always seemed to manage to get out of trouble because his bouncy spirit and enthusiasm moved people to help him (as she was about to do by dropping the lunch off at school).

She smiled as she now thought about the way Eddie and his father, Ted, would banter about baseball, and how delighted she was the time she was called on to be the home-plate umpire as the two of them dramatized how the catcher should have played the bunted ball in the third inning with runners on first and third. Feelings of joy and gratitude welled up within her as she thought of Eddie and Ted, and about Tracy still asleep in the crib upstairs, and about Tiger the cat, sitting on the windowsill nodding stoically to the robins on the lawn.

The Bible had fallen closed on her lap. The God of the Hebrew Scriptures, so loving and so worthy of praise, she now began to realize, was her God and the God of her family. It was not a matter of her being worthy or deserving of God's love; it was a matter of God's simple goodness and beneficence. She knew that, too.

Later, when she dropped off the lunch at school, Sue thanked the principal for passing the lunch along to Eddie and then added a word of thanks to the principal for doing everything possible to make certain the kids were getting a good education.

The next morning, Sue opened the psalms and tried to be a little more disciplined about her reading, because she wasn't sure that she had "prayed" for the full fifteen minutes the morning before. She thought that the lunch incident may have distracted her.

Sometimes we have the impression, as Larry did, that prayer is something we can only do in church, or at least with some book or formula, or at the very least when we are considering something about God. Sometimes we get the feeling, as Sue did, that if we are reading psalms or reciting our favorite prayers or meditating on a passage from the gospels, that any other thoughts must surely be distractions. But if we take time to consider when we have been most prayerful, even if we don't know exactly how the word "prayerful" would be defined by the experts, we may be surprised to realize that in our own experiences, "prayerful times" and "times of prayer" might not exactly coincide.

If we are taking part in group prayer or participating in a liturgical service, then, of course, our commitment is to the community prayer as well as to our own private concerns. And, at such times, our prayer will reflect that commitment. But if we consider the times when we have attempted to pray alone, we may realize that some of our times of prayer have not been very prayerful and that some times of prayerfulness have not been "official" times of prayer.

Larry might give the Holy Spirit a little more cooperation if he took time out more frequently to reflect on what was happening in his life, as he did on the highway after his friend's comment. Of course, Larry would say that he was only "thinking" or "getting his head together," and he would be right; but from another point of view, what he was doing could also be described as praying his experiences.

Larry was honestly searching for the truth in those "incidents" that were beginning to concern him. And in this search, he didn't allow himself to be sidetracked by cheap excuses or to be intimidated by fear or embarrassment. He was searching for the truth, and any time we search for truth, we are really searching for God. Jesus' self-identification as "the Truth" and his description of the Holy Spirit as "the Spirit of Truth" should give us confidence that our search for truth in our life is itself a prayer.

It would also be accurate to say that we can seek to grasp the truth, or meaning, of our life only because we have already been grasped by the Truth. At our moments of struggling to cut through our self-deception, we are like Larry, experiencing what St. Paul describes as the Holy Spirit's praying within us in ways that we do not even know (see Romans 8:26).

As Sue continues to read and reflect on the psalms, she will notice that the psalms themselves directly address God, not only in praise and thanksgiving, but also in frustration and fear, hope and despair, vengefulness, self-pity, and joy. In other words, the prayer form of the psalms conveys all the questions and feelings that arise out of the life experiences of a people striving to understand the meaning and direction of their lives. Sue's praise and thanksgiving for her family and her life join with the sentiments of the psalms in giving thanks to the Creator and Gift-giver of all.

When Sue noticed the forgotten lunch by the door, she was, of course, distracted from reading and thinking about the psalms. But she was not distracted from prayer. During those moments of what she might call distraction, she was actually understanding in a new way some significant experiences of her life. She was distracted from her customary prayer-time agenda, but she was continuing her prayer now in a way that was more personal, more incarnational, more founded in who she was at that moment in the hands of a loving God. Sue's "distraction" could be described as a way of praying her experiences.

On that particular morning, Sue's prayer was predominantly one of joy and gratitude, because her "distractions" led her into memories of happy experiences. On another morning while reading the Psalms, her "distractions" may take her into thoughts about an argument she had with Ted the evening before. If she is not sidetracked by thoughts of self-pity or self-justification or plans to get even but is truthful and open about the experience and honestly seeks to become aware of what the argument providentially calls her to, then her communication with God may include anger and frustration, regret and repentance. And that will be prayer, too, because that will be an honest, if painful, step in the search for truth in her life.

Many great saints have described experiences of prayer, and almost all of these descriptions imply that even during the rare moments of the most advanced prayer, there is always movement along this path of searching for and coming to the truth of who we are in the presence of God. Prayer is not a matter of formulas or pious thoughts; it is a matter of honesty and searching for the meaning, the truth of our experiences, however painful that truth may be.

In praying our experiences, what matters is not so much the particular sentiments that come to us or the pious quality of our thoughts, but our desire to be more and more open to the Truth of the Spirit revealed in the truth of our experiences.

To pray our experiences is not to pray to win or to succeed or to obtain the things we think we need in order to be content and happy. It is not to pray for what is external to our deepest concerns. It is rather to pray for enlightenment and courage and acceptance and gratitude.

Praying our experiences is opening ourselves to God in order to know ourselves as God knows us and to love ourselves as God loves us in the experiences of our life. It is the willingness to accept ourselves as God accepts us and to love ourselves and others as God loves us and them. It is the desire to act in a Christlike way in response to what we will come to know to be God's call in our experiences.

This form of prayer is not worrying or planning or aimlessly daydreaming. It is not devising a strategy or rationalizing about a memory. It is coming to know that we are held in God's infinite love and mercy as that all-encompassing Truth is focused and revealed in our experiences.

Our God is always with us. We come to know God in and through our daily life experiences, because God is the source of our existence, and God's mercy is the very heart of our life. We come to know God by knowing that our life is penetrated and sustained by God's knowledge and love, not only always and everywhere, but also here and now in each particular experience.

This kind of prayer is always possible, but we may not always be attracted to it. Rather, we may be drawn to hear God's word through reflection on a passage of the Scriptures, or we may find ourselves called to simply be attentive to the presence of God. But at times, we may also find ourselves praying our experiences, as did Sue and Larry. Then, hearing the word of God in the events of our daily life, we will be challenged and consoled, confirmed and confronted, judged and ultimately graced with the peace of knowing that the God of history and the universe is truly the God of the mundane experiences of our life as well.

In their own unique ways, Larry and Sue each allowed the Spirit of Truth to bring a new and truth-filled illumination to the experiences of life. To receive this truth, each had to avoid indulging in the preoccupation of the moment or being sidetracked by feelings of fear, self-pity, self-satisfaction, or self-justification. Each accepted the new awareness and responded with honesty.

For Sue, this meant being more conscious of the gifts in her own life and cultivating a sense of gratefulness that began to include all of life. For Larry, it meant being aware of a personal weakness and opening himself to union with God through repentance. For both of them, it meant being grasped by the Spirit of Truth and saying yes to that loving embrace.

3. Obstacles to Praying Our Experiences

Some Considerations about Prayer

Praying our experiences is the practice of reflecting on and entering honestly into our everyday experiences in order to become aware of God's word in them and offer ourselves through them to God. We pray our experiences when we use the content of our lived existence as the content of our prayer. Our memories and desires evoke the concrete happenings of our past, as well as our plans and hopes for the future. These memories, hopes, and feelings are the very focus of our prayer when we pray our experiences.

All of us have probably prayed this way, although we called it by another name. We called it "just thinking" when on a sick-bed we spent restless and empty days pondering the meaning of our pain. We called it "questioning" when after an experience of failure and despair we passed sleepless nights asking why. We called it "resting" when we did nothing of consequence as we vacationed after a particularly stressful period. Yet in retrospect, this time of thinking, questioning, and getting ourselves together might have been as helpful to our faith life as hours of formal prayer. We had indeed been praying our experiences as we unfolded our memories and feelings in the presence of the Lord to see what our day-to-day living might be telling us and to what it might be calling us.

But sometimes our understanding of what prayer "should" be makes us uneasy when our own memories and feelings intrude during a time of prayer. Sometimes we take specific measures to block out memories and feelings, believing that details of our life are not the proper content of prayer. We might have been taught that prayer is a sublime and otherworldly activity in which the everyday has no part. We might have learned that in prayer we should talk to God about God. So we may consider prayer to involve focusing on some kind of mental image of God somewhere in the distance. Consequently, we ordinarily regard reflection on our experiences as an obstacle to prayer, because it connects us to ourselves and seems to prevent our flight to the desired level of communion with God. This is a common but narrow way of viewing prayer.

We have been taught that only as a kind of last resort can our ordinary concerns and experiences be appropriate in prayer. Thus, if the memory of a friend arises during prayer, we might say a brief prayer for the person, but we then return to our "proper" praying. If the memory of a moment of jealousy or pride comes to mind during prayer, if the remembrance of a childhood event or feelings of hurt and rejection fill us, we try to rid ourselves of these distractions and move back to our formal praying. We may even baptize our distractions with a brief moment of prayer if we cannot rid ourselves of them immediately.

Without being fully aware of all the implications, we might have simply defined memories and feelings out of our prayer. We might have named them distractions because we have decided that our prayer for today or for this week will be such and such, and these memories are therefore uncalled for. But consider the contrary: consider the possibility of making these very distractions the content of our prayer—not in order to solve problems or to justify ourselves, not to forward our projects, not to worry, not to plan, not to lick our wounds in self-pity. Rather, we focus on our experiences in order to get in touch with their revelatory power. We hear God's word in them, and we are called to respond.

Praying our experiences is a form of prayer that can be particularly helpful at the end of a busy day. As we come to prayer at that time, our mind is filled with memories of projects and personal encounters. We find ourselves flooded by the pleasant or humiliating feelings that arise from the memories of our behavior. If at this time we try to meditate on one of the mysteries in the life of Jesus or open ourselves simply to the Lord's presence in image-less prayer, we soon find ourselves in an impossible struggle. We recall the harsh words we said so sarcastically during the day. We recall our hurt pride at an admonition, or our anger at not being notified of a schedule change. Or we recall our joy at the phone call from a friend visiting town, or the kindness and patience we extended to a stranger.

If we look upon these recollections as distractions to our prayer, then we will be constantly fighting them. But if we accept them as an integral part of our prayer, then our prayer can take on new aspects and power. We begin to know more clearly both the integrity and the brokenness of our motivation; we can sense more realistically our duplicity; we can become more aware of our goodness; we can see more sharply our values and priorities.

During this type of prayer, we might not generate pious thoughts. We might not read the Scriptures. We might not use theological language. We might not feel that we are resting in the Lord. But in sensing the peace and the call that we know are the signs of yielding to God's presence in our life, we can be sure that we are praying.

Praying our experiences means being open to seeing ourselves as we are and to seeing our personal story as it is known to the Lord. This requires an awareness and an honesty that connects us to our actual daily life. It will lead us to talk to God about ourselves because we are in God's hands, and it will challenge us to growth through purifying self-knowledge. In other words, we will recognize the Divine within ourselves rather than engage in some sublime and otherworldly activity of imagining a God "out there."

Another impression we sometimes have about prayer is that because we pray for the sake of God's glory, we need not be overly concerned if our prayer does not produce any transformation in ourselves. We try to explain away the fact that our prayer is often ineffective in transforming our daily life. Moreover, it seems contrived that various kinds of meditation require that we form a resolution to be carried out during the day for the sake of self-improvement. Praying our experiences, on the contrary, directly addresses the uneasiness we feel at the number of hours we have spent in formal prayer and the small effect these have had on our way of thinking and acting in daily life. In the process of praying our experiences, we resolve this dichotomy between our longing to glorify God and the process of our own transformation. When we pray our experiences, we need not *apply* the meditation to ourselves; the meditation *is* about ourselves, as we hold ourselves before the Lord in an offering of humility and resignation. Here, in our self-knowledge, we find the content of our praise, our thanksgiving, and our offering to God, and we welcome God's transforming power.

4. The Search for Self-Knowledge

Giftedness and Brokenness

Consideration of heavenly things, the imaging of God, or reflection on one of the mysteries of Jesus' life are all important ways into prayer, as is the elimination of all images in the total quiet receptivity of the Lord's presence. However, if we believe that these are the only ways of prayer, we will be eliminating one of the most important paths of prayer—the path of authentic self-knowledge.

St. Teresa of Ávila tried to reconcile our desire to reach God with sublime thoughts and images during prayer and our need and inclination to prayerfully reflect on our life experiences to come to self-awareness in the presence of God. Her conclusion was that we must never close off self-knowledge as a path of prayer, because without it we cannot survive spiritually: "There is no stage of prayer so sublime," she wrote, "that it isn't necessary to return often to the beginning. Along this path of prayer, self-knowledge and the thought of one's sins is the bread with which all palates must be fed no matter how delicate they may be; they cannot be sustained without this bread."[1]

The Lord, we know, desires the intimacy of our offering of ourselves. We sometimes fail to see, however, that this offering is not made in some abstract way with pious words or readings but is established in our welcome of and acceptance of the concrete details of our life as God's providence. The offering of ourselves can only be the offering of our lived experience, because this alone is ourselves. In our prayer we take ourselves into our hands and offer to God our whole self—our strengths and our weaknesses. As Teresa said so simply, "This path of self-knowledge must never be abandoned."[2]

When St. Teresa spoke of self-knowledge, she was not, of course, referring primarily to the self-knowledge that we can learn today from psychological tests. Such tests are useful for their own purposes, but they are based on categories invented by the theoreticians and test makers, and the test results are ultimately comparisons. Rather, Teresa was referring to the self-knowledge that comes to us as we open our heart to God. It is a self-knowledge that is not based on any comparisons; nor does it primarily come from a moralistic critique of ourselves. The self-knowledge that we attain by psychological testing, however helpful, ultimately tells us who we are in the hands of whoever developed the theory and invented the psychological test. The truth that comes to us as we pray our experiences is the unique and incomparable truth of who we are in the hands of God, and who we are called to be in God's continuing providence in our life.

Such self-knowledge frees us into an acceptance and appreciation of our human life as it presently is in all its aspects. Categories we usually apply to our experiences—good and bad, desirable and undesirable, right and wrong—become somehow irrelevant. What is clear is that in God "we live and move and have our being" (Acts 17:28) and that our experiences constitute the story of God's fidelity to us. And we know that that truth is enough.

Authentic self-knowledge is knowledge of our true self and therefore is knowledge of ourselves as we are in relationship to all humankind, to all creation, and ultimately to God. When we speak of authentic self-knowledge, we are referring to the awareness of ourselves as we are in God's arms. There is, therefore, no depth of self-knowledge without a depth of faith. Within this context of faith, self-knowledge grows as we become more aware of both our giftedness and our brokenness. Each of these aspects speaks not only of ourselves but also of God as God relates to us.

Our giftedness speaks to us of God's goodness, because in our giftedness we come to know that we have nothing that we have not received from God (see 1 Corinthians 4:7). In the context of faith, the gifts of our talents, health, and friendships cry out to us of God. If a person believes that the love of a friend is merited, or that purity of motivation is the result of careful planning, that person has only superficial self-knowledge. These are gifts, pure and simple. It is far from the truth to believe that personal holiness can result from proper management of life details or that trust in God is the fruit of personal strategy and effort.

To the extent that we have grown in faith and trust, to that extent we have been gifted. No amount of our own cleverness has produced it. As we grow in self-knowledge, we begin to experience God's blessings—until we at last realize that all of life is a gift.

The awareness of our sinfulness or brokenness also speaks to us of God, for, paradoxically, our sinfulness is also a gift. As Teresa said, "The thought of one's sins is the bread with which

42

all palates must be fed." Our duplicity, our lust, our selfishness, our sloth, our greed, our violence—all speak to us of the fundamental brokenness in our life. We know that no matter what our cleverness or strategies are in the face of this brokenness, we cannot rid ourselves of one speck of duplicity or selfishness, and we sense that our very willfulness in trying to be better is coming from our own self-centeredness. Sometimes we are frightened by the depth of our evil, and we try to ignore it. Yet, in paradox, our sinfulness becomes our bread. In a mysterious way, we can be nourished by our own evil if we accept that evil as part of the truth about ourselves and offer that truth to the Lord.

St. Paul spoke of glorying in his weaknesses (see 2 Corinthians 12:5ff; 11:30; Philippians 3:7ff). He had reached a depth of self-knowledge that permitted him to understand that his righteousness consisted not in freedom from weakness and sin but in being able to say yes to his entire life and his whole self. Paul knew that although a yes to life meant a yes to his own evil, it was also a yes to the God who was sustaining him in the evil with love and drawing him to good. For Paul, the path of faith, not the way of willfulness or works, was the right path to God, because he knew that goodness is a gift of God, not something we can achieve by our own cleverness or effort.

Paul had the boldness to acknowledge that he had done things in the past that he did not want to do and that this ambiguity would continue in the future (see Romans 7:18-19). He knew that he was a sinful person, one who would never reach the imaginary perfection of being faultless. He sought, rather, the authentic Christian holiness of being compassionate and integral, of loving

God and self and neighbor as deeply as he could, of accepting into his self-offering to God his strengths and his weaknesses, his virtues and his sins. Paul offered his total self to God, not only what he would like to be, but what in truth he was. Accepting, appreciating, loving ourselves in truth and offering ourselves in truth is the offering that God asks of us and that forms the basis of prayer.

In one of her letters, St. Thérèse of Lisieux revealed that she shared Paul's insight. "You are mistaken," she wrote, "if you believe that your little Thérèse walks always with fervor on the road of virtue. She is weak and very weak; . . . Jesus is pleased to teach her, as He taught St. Paul, the science of rejoicing in her infirmities. This is a great grace, and I beg Jesus to teach it to you, for peace and quiet of heart are to be found there only."[3]

Thérèse used this awareness as the basis of her "little way." "Perfection seems simple to me," she remarked. "I see it is sufficient to recognize one's nothingness and to abandon oneself as a child into God's arms."[4]

In our brokenness, we come to know God's acceptance and love. In the depths of our heart, we sense God's spirit acting toward healing and integration. That self-knowledge leads us to an awareness of both our evil and God's strength, an awareness that goes beyond what we could know from any theological formula or psychological test. Thérèse acknowledged, "No book, no theologian taught [this Way] to me, and yet I feel in the depths of my heart that I possess the truth."[5] We come to a knowledge similar to what Paul, Mary Magdalene, and Peter had of Jesus and his way with sinners. In faith, self-knowledge leads us to a self-acceptance and a self-love that is enfolded in an awareness of God's love.

Praying our experiences is a way into this depth of authentic self-knowledge, self-acceptance, and self-love. As we embrace our experiences and become aware of our blessedness and our brokenness, we begin to become more aware of the God who fills all of our life with graciousness.

1. *The Book of Her Life,* in *The Collected Works of St. Teresa of Ávila,* trans. Kieran Kavanaugh and Otilio Rodriguez (Washington, DC: ICS Publications, 1976), 94.

2. *The Book of Her Life,* 94.

3. *General Correspondence: Letters of St. Thérèse of Lisieux,* vol. 1, trans. John Clarke (Washington, DC: ICS Publications, 1982, 1988), 641.

4. *General Correspondence: Letters of St. Thérèse of Lisieux,* vol. 2, trans. John Clarke (Washington, DC: ICS Publications, 1982, 1988), 1094; for a slightly different translation see François Jamart, *Complete Spiritual Doctrine of St. Thérèse of Lisieux,* trans. Walter Van De Putte (New York: Alba House, 1961), 134.

5. François Jamart, *Complete Spiritual Doctrine of St. Thérèse of Lisieux,* trans. Walter Van De Putte (New York: Alba House, 1961), 31.

5. SELF-CENTERED REFLECTION

Selfishness and the Limited Ego

In the searching of our experiences, in the unfolding of memories to learn of our weaknesses and giftedness, are we not in danger of focusing on ourselves in a self-centered way? Are we not in further danger of rationalizing and manipulating the memory of our experiences so they tell us what we want to hear? These dangers are, of course, present; but they are dangers on the right road. We must move with some caution but not turn back.

How can we, in this unfolding of experiences, avoid the dangers of self-centered daydreaming and self-justification on the one hand, and rationalizing or even denying our memories on the other? When egoism, denial, and rationalization are already our primary approaches in life, these dangers are quite real—it becomes difficult to avoid selfishness in anything we do, even in our time of prayer. But if we desire to live our life in a spirit of reverence and purity of heart, then reflecting on our experiences will be steeped in this same reverence and purity. The life-stance with which we approach reflection, rather than the reflection itself, is crucial.

In this regard, we may remember being warned against loving ourselves or even against being too concerned about ourselves, lest we fall into a form of selfishness. But we must understand that authentically loving ourselves is not at all selfish, and that if we do not love ourselves, we are seriously weakened in our human and spiritual growth. Authentic love of ourselves is important in our full spiritual development, because it is really our willing acceptance and appreciation of God's love for us. Our love for ourselves is the foundation of our authentic love of others.

In the same way, seeing reflection on our personal story as an obstacle to raising our mind and heart to God is a myopic view. Authentic reflection on life, like authentic love of self, is not the problem but part of the solution.

The very exercise of open and honest reflection on our experiences will, in fact, help us to discern the extent to which selfishness and rationalization control our life-stance. It is a clue that we are indulging in self-centered reflection when we find that our egoism is the source of our energy and that our small world is closing in on us. We then find ourselves judging the memory of our experiences in terms of our ego expectations, and events of our life are labeled good or bad according to our own egotistical standards or those imposed on us. We find ourselves congratulating or reprimanding ourselves depending on whether we have appeared wise or foolish, powerful or weak, clever or obtuse, good or bad. In particular we are certainly egotistical when we defend ourselves by simply blaming or condemning others for our difficulties, or when we find ourselves blaming or condemning ourselves. When we begin to move into this kind of violence toward others or ourselves as we review our experiences, we can be sure we are feeding the ego. Then our reflections are not so much on what our experiences are saying to us as on what we assess to be their value in enhancing our stature as successful persons or in crushing ourselves as failures.

When we make our limited ego the center of our world, we move away from honesty with ourselves and are prevented from being receptive to the truth of our experiences. We close in on ourselves, not because reflection is dangerous, but because our stance is one of egocentrism. When we find ourselves not listening to our total experience but excluding part of it, or evaluating it according to our own expectations, then we can begin to suspect a self-centered stance. When we find ourselves being violent to ourselves or others in our feelings of blame and thoughts of condemnation, then we know we are not on the gospel path of love. When we dissect rather than receive, when we make our reflections ethical considerations of what should be rather than faith-awareness of what is, or when we manipulate our reflections by refusing to enter certain areas of our life—even areas of religious piety and devotion—then to that extent we have placed conditions on our search for God's word in our experiences.

We may also stifle the voice of our experience by controlling our memory and feelings with a refined rationalism. "Can anything good come out of Nazareth?" we ask dismissively, and we do not go to see (see John 1:46). Our rational and analytic thought process becomes a barrier, takes us out of our lived experience, and leaves no crack for the unexpected inspiration or the surprise awareness. We have domesticated God, and our experiences cannot speak the truth to us.

In this way, we may be like the Pharisees pictured in the Scriptures who imposed their rationalism, their egos, and their law on their experience of Jesus. Jesus' words of forgiveness and acts of healing were not seen as manifestations of God's power, because Jesus' acts did not meet the Pharisees' expectations of what the Messiah would and would not do. So, on the basis of their preconception that the Messiah would not associate with sinners, the Pharisees argued that if Jesus were the Messiah, he would know what kind of woman was washing his feet, and he would not allow it (see Luke 7:36-48). Hence, Jesus could not be the Messiah.

The natural feelings of sympathy and admiration that the Pharisees must have had for Jesus were stifled by their preconceptions and expectations. The Pharisees left no room for the unexpected in their experience, and so an awareness of God could not enter.

The Eastern mystical tradition is perhaps more conscious of this difficulty with preconceptions than is the Western popular spirituality. In some forms of Eastern discipline, in order to open the disciple's mind to the nonrational and to the unexpected, the religious master presents the spiritual novice with a koan as the focus for meditation. The koan is a statement or question that makes no sense. It usually includes elements that offer no coherent or reasonable basis from which an analysis can be made. The classic koan "What is the sound of one hand clapping?" contains elements that are themselves in contradiction, and so no reasonable answer by analysis is possible. This is the point. In meditating on the koan, the novice, perhaps after months or years, comes to an awareness that rational analysis and simple logic based on our expectations will not do. The answer, if there is an answer, must come from beyond rationality and analysis, which is to say, from beyond the limited ego.

The understanding of the koan does not come from rationalizing or manipulating the data but emerges in the ego's act of yielding to helplessness. Therefore, it is not a matter of rationally working at the koan that brings awareness. In a similar way, we might say that many of our experiences are themselves koans.

Our experiences, like koans, contain elements that we see as contradictory and as making no sense in terms of our expectations: the death of a beloved child, failure in an area of special competence, a serious injury, falling in love. We ask ourselves for an answer or a meaning. We analyze and reason, but no understanding is forthcoming. Again, that is the point.

It is not by rational analysis or by the manipulation of the data of our experience that understanding and peace will come, but by an egoless reflection in which we open ourselves to a source of power beyond ourselves. It is not by rationally working at the memory of our experiences that we gain awareness and truth; rather, it is by being in faith with our experiences, by taking a welcoming stance toward our life that we grow to a sense of our finiteness and giftedness, and therefore to a sense of God's power and care. Reflecting on our experiences in a reverent way, far from being self-centered, opens us to the source of life on the other side of our limited rational ego.

Discovery and Dialogue

Reflecting on our experiences in an attitude of honesty and discovery is at the heart of the process of praying our experiences. Yet even in our desire to pray, we may sometimes find our reflections deflected by self-centered daydreaming or aimless reminiscing that we know is not on a path of prayer. Our reflections may need a kind of supportive structure to yield a better focus and to put a check on useless mental wanderings. The practice of putting our memories on paper might become for us an important spiritual practice in our willingness to pray our experiences.

The writing of reflections helps us become more conscious of the full dimensions of our experience. It also helps us become more aware of the degree of our selfishness by allowing us to note more objectively where the center of our concerns lies. We cannot write of our experiences for any length of time, or in any depth, without noting what so clearly lies on the paper before us. Recurring judgments, values, and expectations, as well as descriptions of what we take to be our accomplishments and failures, speak to us of our primary life-stance. In our writing, our self-centeredness will surely manifest itself—as will our search for the deeper truth of our life.

At the same time, writing helps us to stop spinning the wheels of our anxiety and prevents us from jumping aboard the merry-go-round of our egotistical daydreaming. If we merely think of our experiences without writing some or all of them on paper, we sometimes find our reflection diffused, scattered, or diverted. We might also find ourselves rethinking the same question a hundred times.

If we are anxious or disturbed about the significance of an experience, the memory tends to return, mushrooming in confusion with each repetition. We begin to feel overwhelmed and disoriented. The experience quickly assumes unmanageable proportions, contaminating other memories. Writing, however, has the power to focus and locate experiences so that they can be put into perspective within our total life and faith context. Juxtaposed in written form, experiences can be reviewed in sequence, pattern, and proportion.

Writing our reflections also gives us an opportunity to move forward at our own pace in the exploration of painful experiences; it allows us simply to list memories and feelings too difficult to be written out or meditated on fully. We may sense that these memories and feelings have a deeper message for us, but they may still be too hurtful to unfold immediately. Our feelings of jealousy or sexuality may be too embarrassing to explore, for example, or the memory of our acts of deceit and sloth too unsettling to consider fully. Even merely listed, the jottings of these experiences and feelings remain as testimonies to our weakness and to our courage. We become aware of our fear and the power that the feelings and memories have over us, but at the same time, we sense a message and know that we will return sometime later to accept it more fully. Having simply named the experience, we know that for the time being we can move on.

Further, writing helps us to open up those experiences and to search through those memories with which we are not immediately comfortable. We begin to see more clearly the patterns of choice leading into the experiences, and the motivations and attitudes undergirding them. Gradually, we become aware of precisely those elements of sinfulness and giftedness in our personal story in which we can especially recognize God's call.

Writing, however, may manifest its greatest power because of its creative and self-generating force. We do not merely put onto paper predetermined words and completed thoughts. Writing has the dynamic, creative character of a movement into the unknown. It cannot fully be choreographed by our intellect, and therefore we can never be sure of what the writing might yield. When we take pen in hand, we grasp a door handle and begin to open areas of our life story and our present awareness that are deeper than we had imagined.

We write more than we are fully conscious of. We may write beyond what we had anticipated, and over the edge of our intellectual awareness. Under our pen emerge reflections and insights and awarenesses that we have not articulated before, but that we have always known to be true at a pre-reflective level.

When we have finished writing or when we reread our writing days or months later, we may say a surprised but honest yes to what we have written. We apparently know much more than we can put into our conscious and orderly thought, and these preconscious understandings emerge as we write and later reread. In writing over the edge of our conscious insights, we often reach a level of awareness that we know to be a gift from God. What opens to us in self-knowledge, we know to be beyond what we could have called forth by our own power.

In writing reflections on our experience, we may also find that we are moved to engage in a kind of conversation or dialogue. We find ourselves addressing the Lord directly in words of contrition and hope: "Lord, I want you; I need you. I am sorry for my wrongdoing; lead me."

And we find ourselves writing a spontaneous reply as from the lips of the Lord: "Why are you afraid? Trust me."

Our conversation continues: "I fear giving in, Lord. I fear my deceit, my pride. I want to trust but cannot."

"You know you can trust; I am with you."

"But I am afraid, Lord; I am afraid to go too far. I want to control my life. I want to organize it."

"Don't you think I can see the deepest desires of your heart?"

"I want you, Lord, to be all in my life, but I hold back."

"You don't have to do everything. I am with you."

As our dialogue continues, we may be surprised by the truths that unfold. Significance and awareness reach a clarity that we had not realized consciously before. We see ourselves in a new light, perhaps in a way we had known in our heart but that we could not articulate before. Conversing with the Lord puts us in touch with depths in our experience that we know to be true in the world of the Lord but that only now rise to conscious awareness. This insight often brings with it great consolation, as we see our life in the hands of God. Yet it may also bring a sense of confrontation as we become aware of the force of our own duplicity. In recognizing now, often vividly, the blessedness of our life, as well as the enormity of our own evil, we experience God's love and God's call.

Prior to our reflection, we might have judged an experience as good or bad, a success or a failure, extraordinary or common; but now labels are no longer significant. We are aware that by judging an experience, we have classified its importance and therefore controlled its impact. In the process of labeling, we have surrendered to the analysis of the ego and have manipulated our experience.

Bad and ordinary experiences, by their very classification, lose meaning and are relegated to marginal consideration. Yet the great liturgical hymn of the Easter Vigil speaks of a *felix culpa*, a "happy fault." Paul referred to glorying in bad experiences, and the gospel speaks of the signs of the kingdom in the most ordinary happenings. Although some events in our life may have more immediate impact than others, and some may make us appear more successful than others, what is important is the realization that every experience has a religious dimension. In essence, every experience embodies the challenge God offers us in love to become more integral and Christlike.

Nothing is more a gift from God than our creation, our life, and our continued existence in God's love. As a gift, our life unfolds under God's loving care. God continually sustains us, graces us, and calls us. Each of our days is a gift and a call from the Creator. To reflect on our experiences, then, is to unwrap the gift, to listen to the call. Far from being a selfish activity, this reflection can be a way of centering on God, a way of hearing God's word addressed to us as individuals in the uniqueness of our person. It can be a way of taking seriously our faith in God's providence and our belief that everything is grace.

The words of the modern Trappist monk Thomas Merton are reassuring. In *Contemplative Prayer*, Merton writes that

> our knowledge of God is paradoxically a knowledge not of God as the object of our scrutiny, but of ourselves as utterly dependent on God's saving and merciful knowledge of us. . . . We know God in and through ourselves in so far as God's truth is the source of our being and God's merciful love is the very heart of our life and existence.[1]

"By meditation," Merton remarks, "I penetrate the inmost ground of my life, seek the full understanding of God's will for me, of God's mercy to me, of my absolute dependence upon God."[2]

Merton describes the aim of prayer much as we have described the aim of praying our experiences: "to come to know God through the realization that our very being is penetrated with God's knowledge and love for us." We know God, Merton adds, "in so far as we become aware of ourselves as known through and through by God."[3] Here Merton describes prayer not so much as our coming to know God or as our seeking to love God, but rather as rejoicing in the truth that we are known and loved by God. That realization rises vividly to consciousness as we enter into the process of praying our experiences.

The eminent Jesuit scholar Karl Rahner, in *Christian at the Crossroads*, puts the matter clearly when he suggests that thinking of prayer as a dialogue with God is difficult to conceive if we understand dialogue to mean messages uttered by God as an outside source. Sudden impulses and insights in prayer, Rahner reminds us, might be explained as coming from our own psychic powers. For many persons, therefore, the notion of dialogue in prayer seems to be the same as talking to ourselves.

Rahner suggests that the notion of prayer as a conversation with God can be more intelligible if we understand that "in prayer we experience ourselves as the ones spoken by God, as the ones arising from and decreed by God's sovereign freedom in the concreteness of our existence." In this way of understanding prayer, "we are ourselves . . . the utterance and address of God which listens to itself."[4] In *Contemplative Prayer*, Merton expresses the same notion when he remarks, "I am myself a word spoken by God."[5]

This means that in prayer we are neither dialoguing with an outside source who utters messages from without, nor are we simply talking to ourselves. We are reaching deeply into ourselves and sensing more clearly that we are in God's knowledge and love. We are discovering the Divine within us. We are creatively experiencing ourselves and our lives as uttered by God, and we listen.

This listening is not a self-centered activity, because we are not simply listening to our own limited ego. Rather, we are opening ourselves to that dimension of our being and experience in which

God speaks. We are not talking to ourselves in such a way that we are consciously controlling and manipulating our reflection.

When we speak of prayer as dialogue, then, we are referring to encountering those levels of ourselves and of our experiences that we do not control because we have not formed them. They are not ours. We do not, in fact, even realize their existence until they manifest themselves. We do not possess these levels of experience; rather, at these levels we are possessed—possessed by God's deep, abiding love. The ego in self-centeredness cannot enter here, for the ego carries the baggage of ambition and fear, of defensiveness and schemes, which cannot be allowed at this level of self-knowledge.

In the Book of Genesis, God utters the word and creation springs forth. Today we are that word. Each of us is uttered in the uniqueness and actuality of our personal story. Our task is to hear that word as it wells up in us from our being and experience. We listen to the word with love and reverence as we let it speak from our depths. Of what does the word speak? It speaks of the giftedness of our life; it speaks of the brokenness of our life. It fills us with awe of God's blessings, and it calls us to deeper purity and love toward God and all creation. But, fundamentally, it speaks to us of God's love. It reverberates with the word of the Scriptures, which often helps us on our journey inward, but it now touches us in our own unique and historical reality.

1. Thomas Merton, *Contemplative Prayer* (Garden City, NY: Doubleday and Company, Image Books, by special arrangement with Herder and Herder, 1971), 83.

2. Merton, 68.

3. Merton, 83.

4. Karl Rahner, *Christian at the Crossroads* (New York: Seabury Press, 1975), 66.

5. Merton, 68.

7. Praying through Scripture

Biblical Events and Our Experiences

In the Christian tradition, all of the Scriptures are sacred to us, but only a small fraction stir and capture us. Some passages arouse in us such an emotional reaction that they cry out to be heard, and we cannot be free of them. These passages have such power over us because they touch a part of us that reverberates with their message. These passages move us, not because they are special in themselves, but because they have connected with a part of ourselves formed by an experience now struggling to be unfolded. Scripture passages that might have meant little to us before suddenly become a powerful force because they light up and refocus our experiences.

The incident of Philip in the Gospel of John (1:43-46) illustrates how an experience can be illuminated by the Scriptures. Philip had no doubt read the Torah with reverence from his youth; yet only after his experience of encountering Jesus did the Scriptures come alive for Philip and refocus the real meaning of his experience. Indeed, the Scriptures became the light illuminating Philip's experience of Jesus. Until then, the Scriptures had lacked the compelling force that they now possessed for him. Then Philip sought out Nathanael, with whom he shared his enthusiasm: "We have found him about whom Moses in the law and also the prophets wrote, Jesus son of Joseph from Nazareth" (John 1:45).

Another case in which the Scriptures illuminated the depths of an experience is the account of the two disciples on the road to

Emmaus (Luke 24:13-35). After that terrible and disheartening Friday, they were downcast. A stranger who had caught up to them as they walked consoled them by recalling to them passages from the Scriptures that referred to the Messiah. "Then beginning with Moses and all the prophets, he interpreted to them the things about himself in all the scriptures" (Luke 24:27). No doubt the disciples had heard these Scriptures before without being captured by them. Even now, although they listened intently, they were not aware of the compelling power the word was having on them. But after they had recognized Jesus, the Scriptures smoldering in their hearts flamed out, and they realized that their hearts had been burning within them as the stranger spoke with them and explained the Scriptures to them. The Scriptures had illuminated and refocused that profound Friday experience for the two disciples, and they ran to tell the others.

As we read the Scriptures, some passages enkindle our hearts. Our emotional response is our clue that a particular passage is addressed to us in a special way at this time in our life. We might have read the passage a hundred times before, but now it arouses us and calls us clearly and decisively. We are ready to be led into the depths of an experience, and the Scriptures will serve as our light.

Both for Philip and for the disciples on the road to Emmaus, the Scriptures served as a light on their experience. They could then turn from the Scriptures to explore and treasure their experience. They found in a literal way in their experience what we in faith also encounter: the presence and the call of the Lord. As with Philip and the disciples, the Scriptures serve us by illuminating, clarifying, and evaluating our experiences. Often, like a true friend, the Scriptures reach into our hearts to arouse and to console by bringing out into the open memories, feelings, and desires that we might scarcely have known were there.

These memories and feelings and longings become the passage into the presence of Christ in our life. They resonate with the call of God. The Scriptures arouse us, not to focus on the scriptural passages themselves, but to open ourselves to Christ, who lives in us and walks with us today. We believe that the Holy Spirit, whom Jesus promised to send to us, is the primary author of the Scriptures. That same Spirit is today the primary author of our own life and continues to author all of creation. We are the co-authors of our life, and as St. Paul assures us over and over, we live "in Christ" today.

Sometimes our respect for the Scriptures is so profound that we feel uneasy as we turn our attention from them to our experience. But in respecting them as a privileged expression of the word of God, we should not fail to respect also our own experience as a privileged expression of that same word of God. When we realize that the Scriptures themselves were written out of the experiences of the sacred authors and the community, we begin to view the events in our own life with more reverence. The God who is revealed through the events recounted in the Scriptures is also revealed in our daily life. This awareness makes less problematic our reflection on personal experiences as a way of knowing God's present word for us.

The sacred Scriptures were written within a given culture for a particular audience with a specific theological language and imagery. The world we live in has changed dramatically since the Scriptures were composed, and so we cannot expect our experiences of God to duplicate those recorded in the Bible. Our experiences today have the mark of our personal and communal lives within a particular culture at a particular time. But we can expect the sacred writings to shed light on our experiences and to help us explore and critique them.

The people of Israel sometimes confused their religious belief that God was faithful with their more rational expectation that God would be consistent with their own understanding of God and history. We sometimes fall into the same trap. We can expect our experiences of God's call in our life to be in accord with God's call to Israel, but we would do ourselves an injustice to assume that there will be no surprises in our life. One of the consistent elements of God's call to Israel was the invitation to accept precisely the unexpected: "Your ways are not my ways" (Isaiah 55:8, NJB).

Another consistent element of God's call is God's own love and fidelity. God will always be faithful to us; God will forever hold us in love. But we would be mistaken to assume that God will meet our expectations. The ways of God's love and fidelity are always creative and so necessarily will not be what is expected. Hope founded on personal trust and love, not expectation coming from the limited ego, is our needed response.

A closed attitude to how God might be present in our life forces us to do violence to our experiences, just as such a closed attitude caused the Pharisees to reject and do violence to their experience of Jesus. Their misguided allegiance to a narrow understanding of the Scriptures and tradition resulted in their missing God, present among them. The Pharisees assumed that any experience of the Messiah would fit their understanding of the Scriptures. They filtered personal experience through their superficial reading of the holy word. We can be victims of the same dangerous possibility if we fail to open ourselves to receiving the Lord in our daily life.

Mary and the apostles read the same holy writings as the Pharisees, but they did not use the writings to prejudge their experiences. Mary and the apostles placed a supreme value on being available whenever and however God might call. In practice, they came to reverence their experiences, and they allowed them to become the path along which they walked with the Lord.

The Scriptures serve us best, not when they become a filter through which we prejudge our experiences, but when they become our light and mirror. As our light, the Scriptures help us to clarify and refocus our experiences. As our mirror, they help us to explore and discover aspects of our experiences that previously had been inaccessible to our gaze. Neither a light nor a mirror is used to best advantage if it is looked at for its own sake. Rather, both are most helpful as means of illuminating and exploring. If we find ourselves using the Scriptures as an excuse for not exploring and treasuring our own experiences, then we can suspect that we do not understand the very best of the good news: that God is lovingly present to us in our daily living.

By praying our experiences, we come to know God's loving action in the here and now of our daily life. We can then begin to focus on these experiences as the content of our offering to the Lord. Frequently the Scriptures will enlighten us to the importance of an experience and move us into the depths of meaning that that experience might have for us. The Scriptures, however, will be misused in prayer if they cause us to do violence to our experiences or to place no value on them. But if we use passages of the Scriptures to lead us back to our actual experiences, to illuminate them and to enlighten us to explore and treasure them, we may in this way come closer to an awareness of God's action—Christ's life—in our life today.

8. INCARNATIONAL PRAYER:

Praying from Our Humanness

At the heart of Christian prayer resides the central mystery of Christianity, the incarnation: "The Word became flesh and lived among us" (John 1:14).

The incarnation holds this central place in prayer, not only in the sense that we pray to God through and in and with the Word-made-flesh, but also because our own humanness, having been taken on by the Son of God, is the womb of our prayer. As Christ Jesus, now seated at the right hand of God, continues to share all the aspects of humanity with God, so our own sharing with God flows out of our human life. As Christ Jesus is united with God in humanness, we are drawn by the Spirit of Jesus to God in our humanness. The meaning and the hope of the mystery of the incarnation, consummated in the resurrection-ascension, point to the truth that humanness is incorporated into Godness.

Through the incarnation, human life becomes for God an experience. God is not a spectator to human life but knows us in the biblical sense of knowing through intimate experience. God knows human life not only from having created it but from having lived it. The Word by which creation took place became flesh in order to enjoy and to agonize as a human being, to play and to cry, to experience the life and death patterns of humans in the midst of creation. The mystery of the incarnation assures us that God is at home in humanness, and the mystery of the resurrection-ascension further assures us that humanness is at home in the Godhead.

"The Word became flesh and lived among us." It is clear in the gospel that the Son of God lived human life, not in some kind of pretense or in an otherworldly style, but "in the flesh." An early Christian heresy held that Jesus only looked like a human being, that he posed as a man. Very few hold that idea today, but too few reflect on what it might mean that the Son of God experienced human life with all its messiness and sadness and fear, as well as its love and joy and beauty.

What might these considerations have to do with our prayer?

For many of us, in our efforts to develop our relationship with God, humanness seems to be part of the problem. We wish that we did not have human difficulties. We wish that we did not need to struggle with this or that part of the human condition. We might wish we were someone else, someone more noble or important, someone less weak and unworthy. Sometimes we might even wish that parts of ourselves would simply cease to exist—that we could just blot out certain parts of ourselves and our experiences. We want to rise above our humanness. We take the soaring impulses of our spirit to mean that our humanness, with all its finiteness, stupidity, and foolishness, is too limited and too ungodly to be of value. There is often a curious and subtle wish to be angelic.

Sometimes we deny our humanness; sometimes we reject our humanness; mostly we are quietly afraid of it—of the uncontrollability of its demands, of its limitations and brokenness, and of its inevitable slide to death. We are simply embarrassed about our humanness and wish that it would go away. We wish that our human concerns were over so that we could pray.

But the incarnation tells us that our subtle desire to become angelic and rid ourselves of human concerns is a way of not meeting the Word on the Word's own ground: human life. The mystery of the incarnation means that human concerns are concerns to God, and that our task is to accept and appreciate human life as human life and not to reject it as lesser angelic life. Jesus came that we would have this human life with abundance, not with embarrassment or fear or reluctance.

Christian prayer, then, is not an attempt to move out of mundane human life but rather to enter into it more fully (see John 10:10). Both the way of our prayer and the content of our prayer are to be not otherworldly but very much this-worldly. That is why, perhaps, one of the earliest Christian traditions about prayer spoke of it as not having been finished until the lips moved. That also may be why the earliest Christian forms of prayer were so involved with the physical: gestures, bodily movements, pilgrimages, processions, all surrounded with the sensualness of icons, candles, incense, and the touching of statues and beads.

We may look at these practices as primitive or unsophisticated, but we cannot afford to lose the fleshiness, the incarnationality, of our prayer. Some forms of prayer—for example, trying to rid ourselves of all our thoughts of human concerns so as to think only of God—may be a way that we vent our feelings of embarrassment about our human life. We sometimes suppose that prayer has to do with having wonderful ideas about

God. But if our prayer is the raising of our human mind and our human heart to God, then we can hardly presume that our prayer will contain only lofty thoughts.

The reality of the Word's having become flesh and having lived among us assures us that God is at home in human experience and that our prayer is born from our human experience. In particular, it suggests that, at least at certain times in our life or in certain circumstances, we may find that the contents of our prayer, what we share with God in prayer, what is on our mind and in our heart raised to God, will be founded in our human experience, not in something otherworldly.

Jesus' own teachings on prayer emphasizes that if prayer is not to be hypocritical, it must come from our heart—that is, from the center of our being, from the reality of our life—rather than only from our lips. Prayer originating in the heart may do well to end up on the lips, but prayers originating on the lips can be merely words without heart—that is, without the concrete reality of our life (see Matthew 15:8; Mark 7:6). Jesus assured his disciples that when they prayed, they did not need to heap words on words as the pagans did, for what is more important is not the abundance or even the precision of the words, but that the words carry the heart. It is the heart raised to God that matters.

The Hebrew Scriptures speak of God as not needing sacrifices of burnt offerings or holocausts of any kind but longing for the offering of a contrite and humble heart (see Psalm 51:17-19; Hebrews 10:8; Micah 6:6ff). God's request that we offer our heart is, of course, a personal invitation to return love for love. The point of prayer is to offer to God our authentic selves. The heart, contrite and humble, is a symbol of that open, honest, loving sharing with God of the essence and totality of who we really are.

The story of the disciples on the road to Emmaus is a fine example of what praying our experiences might be for us who are disciples of the Word-made-flesh, as we go our way on the road of life (see Luke 24:13-35). The risen Jesus comes to us as he did to those original disciples on the road to Emmaus, unrecognized; and taking the initiative, he asks us to share with him the concerns of our life: "What are you discussing as you go your way?" We, like those disciples, may resist, because like them, we may be confused or embarrassed about our foolish or cowardly role in those concerns.

The disciples were distressed. They did not want to share their story, and their feelings of resistance expressed themselves in the form of a counterquestion: "Are you the only one who does not know the things that have happened in Jerusalem?" But Jesus was not to be resisted. He insisted, "What things?"— "Tell me about yourself; let me share your distress, your confusion, all aspects of your experience; let me hear your story, so that I can increase your faith and trust." And when the disciples began to share their humanness with Jesus and hear his reply, their hearts, their very selves, were ignited. They were filled with faith and became proclaimers of faith in the risen Christ.

What Jesus asks of his disciples in this story is what he seems to ask constantly of us in his desire for intimacy; that is, that we share with him our concerns, our feelings, the events of our life—that we pray our experiences. We deepen our relationship with God in prayer by sharing with God what, in fact, is happening in our human life.

We say the Lord's Prayer for world peace, we offer a Hail Mary for a sick friend, we say the Serenity Prayer to help us through the next hour, or we pray a psalm in thanksgiving for a special grace. But praying our experiences particularly focuses on exploring with the risen Lord, as simply as did the disciples on the road, the significance of the events of our life and how we are called to respond. We share with the Word-made-flesh our own experience of what it is to be fleshy.

The reality of the incarnation assures us that human concerns are God's concerns, and it therefore invites us to look upon our prayer as a lifting to God of our mind and heart filled with those human concerns. From our humanness, our prayer is born. In prayer, empowered by the Spirit of Truth, we share our story with the Lord as did the disciples on the road to Emmaus. Perhaps at first, we share it with some inner struggle. But then, with a deepening self-knowledge, we come to an acceptance of our experiences, and finally we are graced with an appreciation and gratitude for our life and ourselves as we really are in the hands of God. Then we, like the disciples, can authentically respond in action by proclaiming faith in the Word-made-flesh, now risen and seated at the right hand of God.

9. PRAYING OUR STORY

Enfolding Our Story into God's Story

The disciples on the road to Emmaus were distressed (see Luke 24:13-35). Driven by fear and discouragement, they were fleeing from their misery. Jesus, the stranger, aware of their suffering, stopped them and initiated a conversation that would lead them to regain their inner freedom and to experience inner healing.

Jesus asked the disciples simply, "What are you discussing as you go your way?" The question was disturbing, and at first the disciples resisted, but Jesus insisted, gently repeating his invitation. Then the disciples shared their story, a story of some success and much pain, of expectations and disappointments, but mainly a story of deep hurt, discouragement, sadness, and fear. Jesus embraced their story with the compassion of his presence, assuring them that their story needed to be seen in the light of faith. "Beginning with Moses and all the prophets," Jesus now retold the story of God's faithful, loving presence to their ancestors, and therefore really retelling their own story as it had developed over the centuries. And with the gentle love of the faithful God described by the prophets, Jesus enfolded the disciples' distressing story—their bleeding hearts, really—into God's story of healing and deliverance.

Although they did not seem to realize it, the disciples were in bondage, in the unfreedom and oppression of their feelings of discouragement and fear. Jesus now assured them, by sharing God's story revealed by Moses and the prophets, that God's story was a story of liberation and freedom. The disciples did not need to be in bondage. The story of Moses and the prophets told them that their ancestors—and they themselves by that ancestry—had been chosen and loved by God and that God was with them in their confusion and suffering, leading them to freedom.

The disciples felt shame and guilt for having abandoned Jesus in his darkest hour—the disciples had been unfaithful to Jesus. But Moses and the prophets had taught that God was always faithful and never vengeful.

The disciples also felt abandoned by their friend and leader, Jesus. They needed to know more deeply that they were loved and treasured and would never be abandoned by God. Moses and all the prophets had proclaimed that important truth also: that God would never forget them or abandon them but would treat them as beloved children.

The disciples were confused and disappointed, their expectations in ruins. Moses and the prophets had told them that God's ways were not their ways but that God's providence surrounded them even in their misery.

By sharing with the disciples the story of God's work on behalf of their ancestors and thus God's work in the world and in their lives, Jesus opened God's story and welcomed them into it. By presenting the teachings of Moses and the prophets, Jesus reminded the disciples of the important eternal truths that were revealed to their ancestors and were now flowing into their own lives. And these truths ignited the hearts of the disciples, their faith rekindled by the Holy Spirit. They recalled in grateful amazement, "Were not our hearts burning within us as he talked to us and opened the Scriptures to us?" In their honest conversation with Jesus, the stranger, and in their willingness to see their story embraced into God's story, the disciples were praying their experiences.

Although they may not have realized it at the time, the two disciples had already on other occasions had the experience of enfolding their story into God's story. Before that fateful Good Friday, the disciples had participated many times in the Passover meal as members of the Israelite community. The Passover ritual was Israel's most important traditional prayer ceremony, in which the people told God's story and their story, remembering all that God had done for them. In reality, the two disciples on the road, as they shared their own story, were involved in the same kind of interaction with the stranger, Jesus, as they had been in their interaction with the liberating God each time the community told their story in the communal Passover ritual.

In recalling their stories, the community of Israel and the two disciples were not, of course, engaging in an academic exercise of recounting history. Rather, in remembering their stories, they were praying, reaching out for a richer understanding of truth and meaning, seeking renewed hope and trust, as well as celebrating the faith they already had.

As we explore our own experiences in truth, we discover that our story is not unlike the story of the disciples on the road, or the story of Israel told in the Passover ritual. We find ourselves in bondage as did the Israelites, who were captives in Egypt, and as did the disciples, who were in the clutches of fear and discouragement. Our bondage is not physical slavery, but the unfreedom of fear, sin, shame, and guilt. We find ourselves driven by our anxieties and excessive feelings of unrest, crushed by our failed expectations, cowed by stirrings of shame for our cowardice, and intimidated by discouragement and guilt for sometimes fleeing from our deepest call.

Sometimes we are like the original wanderers in the desert, roaming in the desert of confusion and emptiness; sometimes we are like the disciples, running from our pain and not knowing exactly where we are going. Our life is in disarray; our prayer, thinly veiled complaints. We want to return to our previous security. We resist the invitation to stop and regain the meaning of our life in prayer. We have very little to follow—only the vague hope that it might all make sense one day. Then God becomes for us the stranger with compassion and challenge, or the pillar of fire by night and the cloud by day, leading us to a place that we did not know.

Later, like Israel, we may joyfully remember the desert experience; and like the disciples on the road, we may gratefully retell the story of our Emmaus journey, in which we returned to our inner freedom. Later, when seen in the context of God's overall story, the most painful and confusing aspects of our story may glow as providential. We know we are the better for having lived as honestly and as courageously as we could through the struggle, even as we headed down the wrong path and complained. We now know more about ourselves, and especially about God's compassion in dealing with us and with the world. We may even celebrate in prayer and liturgy some aspects of that distressing period of our life, as did Israel in the Passover ritual and as did the disciples in the Eucharist with their risen Lord.

As we pray our experiences, we open ourselves not only to hope but also to transformation. Jesus' challenge to us is the same as his challenge to Israel and to the disciples on the road: conversion—*metanoia*, to turn around, to let go of our bondage to fear, to come back to the inner freedom of our best self, to see new dimensions in our experiences, to change our heart (see Mark 1:14-15). Jesus assures us that the Spirit of Truth will teach us and empower us to be transformed. To come to the truth, to have a change of heart—a burning heart—as did the disciples on the road, is to have our story transformed, re-created by the Spirit. In this way we experience our prayer to be the gift of the Spirit in us (see Romans 8:26-27).

By praying their experiences, the Israelites and the disciples on the road focused not only on the pain of the past but also on the hope of transformation in the future. As the understanding of their past grew and developed in faith, their understanding of themselves and of their God grew. The God who had given them the past and who had blessed them in the present would lead them into the future as well. Of this, "Moses and all the prophets" were certain. Neither Israel nor the disciples needed to be afraid; God would not abandon them.

When Jesus, the greatest of the prophets and priests, celebrated the Passover, its meaning opened out into the future in a gloriously new way. Jesus celebrated the Passover by reliving it, and the future broke into the present reign of God, making resurrection possible. The disciples on the road, participating in the paschal mystery with the Lord revealed in the breaking of the bread, rejoiced, their eyes now opened. They got up and went immediately to share themselves and their story—now transformed— with the others staying in Jerusalem.

When we pray our story, we, too, find ourselves called into transformation and the promise of the future. We not only remember the past as past, but we see the past as holding a glorious but overlooked present reality, as well as a glorious future potential. Like the disciples, we find that the God who has been with us in creation and in the Eucharist is present to us now through continuing providence and is leading us into the potential of resurrection. The Spirit reveals who we are called to be by enfolding our story of giftedness and weakness into the tenderness and healing of God's story of providence and promise. We experience our poverty; we experience our blessedness; we experience our call to act; we experience God's welcoming and ever-embracing goodness.

By praying our story, we hear our call to become more fully available to God's love and more filled with God's power and graciousness. The God of creation, of the exodus, of the incarnation, of the Eucharist, of resurrection, and of continuing providence, having led us to the present, will be with us in the future in transforming power. Thus, in the presence of the resurrected Jesus and empowered by the Spirit, we get a glimpse of who we are called to be and what we are called to do.

In the process of praying our story, then, we bring together our past and our future into the present moment of experiencing the freedom, compassion, and healing power of God. All of our giftedness and all of our painful past, as well as all of our hoped for and sometimes dreaded future, are gathered into the present moment of our confusion and joy, before the God who has been with us from the beginning, sustaining and loving us. As our story is enfolded into the loving, merciful providence of God's story, the truth of our identity and our call is revealed to us. Then, welcoming the reality of God's love in our life, we can say without fear but with honesty and inner freedom, with surrender and gratitude, what the disciples said to the stranger on the road, "Stay with us, because it is almost evening" (Luke 24:29).

10. Being Available to God as We Are

True Self and False Self

As the disciples on the road to Emmaus were at first reluctant to accept Jesus' invitation to share their story, we sometimes also find it difficult to honestly reflect on our experiences. Some experiences are distressful or disappointing, and then there is the temptation to change some aspects of our story to our own advantage. In our tendency toward self-protection and self-promotion, we reflect on our experiences as we wish they were or as we wish we were. We deny the reality of who we are, we want to be someone else, and we reject the person we are called to be. In our deceit and selectivity, we adjust our story to feed our need for self-flattery, to interpret our story as an act of our powerful ego.

On the contrary, when we pray our experiences honestly, we seek the truth of who we are in the truth of each of our experiences and in the truth of all of them in relationship to one another and within the truth of God's love and providence.

The truth, of course, is that we are loved by God and are in union with God, that God knows and loves us with an infinite knowledge and love, that God is always pressing toward us and is always available to us. The truth is that all of creation lives and moves and has existence in God (see Acts 17:28). The truth is that in our sinfulness and weakness we are utterly dependent on God; that we are filled with confusion and self-seeking;

that we are in bondage to our compulsions and drives; that our addictions, fears, and hurts cover us in blindness and trap us in violence and unfreedom. The truth is that we are in need of liberation and redemption.

Our need for redemption is the truth that we resist in our self-protective stance and in our desire to be self-righteous, to be worthy in our own eyes, to be secure, and to be established in our own identity. Our need for redemption is the truth that will set us free, and yet, paradoxically, we resist that truth, because our present bondage to our own self-centeredness and self-promotion gives us the illusion of being free already. We believe that we are free because we can do what we want; but we are blind to the reality that we do not want what is really in the interest of our true self. We do not want what we are really called to be and to do.

When we make our true self available to God in praying our experiences, we acknowledge our total dependence on God and open ourself to transforming grace. However, when we bring to God only the false self fashioned by our own self-centeredness, we block God's efforts in us. The false self has as its priority our egotistical interests, ambitions, and glory.

The difference between the false self and the true self is illustrated in the parable of the Pharisee and the publican, which Luke tells us Jesus addressed precisely to those who were self-righteous (Luke 18:9-14). Our false self is symbolized by the Pharisee, who goes to the temple to pray, ostensibly to bring his story before God. But instead of praying his experiences, he distorts his story, telling God only how good he is, how much he has kept the law.

He relies on comparison and violently condemns the publican who is in the back of the temple.

The Pharisee's way of reflecting on his experiences is not prayer. He makes his story an occasion for self-justification, self-righteousness, and condemnation of another. He may be telling a partial factual truth, but he fails to see the whole truth. He does not realize the deepest truth of his heart: that his story is really the story of God's empowerment and love in him. By failing to pray his story in complete honesty, he blocks his ability to be compassionate and loving, and he blindly thanks God that he is not like the rest of sinners. He does not see his own sinfulness—the sinfulness that blinds him to God's goodness in him and makes him violently condemn the publican. The Pharisee has distorted his story for the sake of his own interest, thereby cutting himself off from the God of truth and from a true relationship with others.

Our false self is also ever ready to barter truth for flattery, power, and security. It is determined to sacrifice honesty for self-promotion. It exploits our resources on behalf of our personal agenda. The false self puts our giftedness at the service of our ego and would squander our gifts and talents for acclaim and good feelings. It is the self of fear and deception. It is the self of violence and self-righteousness, which is not in touch with the deepest realities of our heart.

Our false self is made up of fear and duplicity, crystallized in that most grievous of all lies, which erupts in our piety as the pharisaical need to make worthiness, self-righteousness, and self-justification the basis of our security, our self-worth, even our so-called prayer and holiness. The false self undermines prayer, because it denies the one fundamental truth that establishes our relationship with God: our absolute dependence on God's love. The Pharisee, the false self, had no need for a love relationship with God; he needed only to report to God on his self-promoting progress, as a clerk might report to a superior accountant.

Our true self is symbolized by the publican. The publican does not rely on his own worthiness as he presents himself to God; worthiness is not his concern. He does not consider his own self-achieved goodness or holiness; he has none. He does not look to his state of perfection for credentials to be before God. Rather, "keeping his distance," he humbles himself before God and, not comparing himself with anyone, keeps his distance also from the Pharisee, his would-be adversary. He does not have an agenda of self-flattery. He has no credentials, no security, no worthiness, and no righteousness. He does not support himself by condemning anyone and has no need to build his virtue on anyone else's weakness. He has only his willingness to be who he is before God. The publican's prayer is not a report to an accountant on his self-promoting progress; instead, he makes himself available in honesty to his God. From his place in the back of the temple, he prays his experiences with simple and profound self-awareness and with the deepest truth of his heart.

The publican's security is his honesty before God, and he has the courage and trust to let that be enough. His hope is not based on the rightness of his condition but on his faith in the compassion of God and on his willingness to receive it. His prayer does not consist of a comparison with anyone else; rather, it is himself alone—his own true story—that he brings before God.

As in the parable, our false self struggles against our true self to win our heart and to tell our story. Sometimes we experience this struggle in a fleeting moment when, in recounting an incident to a friend, we find ourself justifying or distorting the factual truth in such a way that we appear right or better. Or we may experience this struggle when we find ourself selectively avoiding a part of our story when we come to pray. We withhold from our prayer a particular relationship or behavior that we are afraid to expose. Indications such as these make us aware that our false self may be adjusting our story. These tendencies to distort and be selective with our experiences may be so deep in us that we are not fully conscious of them at the time but only later come to see them. Then that awareness itself is a great grace of the Spirit of Truth.

Our false self and our true self play out the drama of the Pharisee and publican within us—a drama that actually becomes our unique and lifelong spiritual path. Our path is unique, because our particular gifts and weaknesses are the resources of our true self while, at the same time, they are exploited by our false self. And it is lifelong, because we will be experiencing our tendencies toward weakness and sinfulness and our subtle self-centeredness and self-protection even on our deathbed.

If the Pharisee had had his way, he would have violently ejected the sinful publican from the temple. The publican, however, not needing to be an adversary to anyone, confident of God's mercy, and aware of his own sinfulness, was not disturbed by the presence of the Pharisee. And that is the way it is with our false self and our true self.

Our true self does not need to be defensive and certainly does not need to attack our false self. We do not need to become violent against those parts of ourself that form and manifest our false self. And if we experience our false self as the enemy, then we need to know that Jesus has told us to treat our enemy with love (see Matthew 5:44). We are not to give way to our enemy; rather we are to keep our distance, to stand our ground without hostility and without fear but with inner freedom and creative love. We can leave the inevitable spontaneous disruptions of our false self to God's providence in our surrender to our spiritual path.

At the moment we recognize and begin to accept the depth of brokenness in ourselves, the adversarial relationship of our false self against our true self takes an ironic turn. We recognize our false self as part of who we really are, and we begin in our prayer the long process of welcoming and creatively healing that false self. We do not need to fear our false self or make our false self an adversary. We can acknowledge our weaknesses and even accept our false self as part of our fundamental weakness, not because of our strength, but because of God's strength in us. With Paul, we have the sense that if we will glory in anything it will be in our weakness (see 2 Corinthians 11:30; 12:5ff; Philippians 3:7ff).

Our story now takes on new dimensions of truth. We now more consciously and more fully entrust to the Lord not only our false, self-centered actions, but also our false self in all of its weakness, sinfulness, and brokenness. In this honest stance of our true self, we become present to the transforming power of God's healing, forgiving, and redeeming love.

The Spirit of Truth establishes our true self. The false self would house us in the presence of our self-denial and self-deception and not in the presence of God. Our willingness to be at home in the presence of God allows the Spirit of Truth already within us to empower us to no longer need to be dominated by or even concerned about the false self.

As we become more available to receiving God's love—that is, as we become more open to welcoming the Holy Spirit—we become more profoundly aware and receptive of our union with God and of our emptiness before God. This stance of total dependence on God's infinite goodness allows us to share the prayer of the publican. He prays his experiences by being who he is in the truth of God's love and his own sinfulness. He prays simply, "Lord, be merciful to me, a sinner."

The publican asks for God's mercy. It is a profound, redeeming prayer, because it opens the publican to God, the source of infinite mercy. When we speak of God's mercy and love, it sometimes sounds as if God has mercy and love as commodities and dispenses them like a pitcher dispenses juice. But love and mercy are not separate from God. God *is* love (see 1 John 4:8). We cannot receive God's mercy and love without receiving God. God answers the publican's prayer, not by giving him a "cupful" of love, but by enfolding the publican in God's own essence of Love and Mercy.

The publican's prayer is the simple prayer of being totally available to God. The publican prays that God will embrace him—a sinner—into the essence of God, who *is* Love and Mercy. In particular, the publican's prayer is the prayer of loving God by welcoming the Holy Spirit, God's Love in the Trinity, into the publican's own life. In this prayer, Love settles into the publican, becoming his own self-acceptance and self-love; Love flows through the publican back to God, becoming the publican's own continuing prayer; and Love flows outward in charity to others, specifically to the Pharisee, enabling the publican to not retaliate and to not make the Pharisee *his* enemy.

Jesus calls us to make the publican's prayer our prayer, so that we, too, ask God to be God in our life; so that we, too, accept God as our Lord; so that we, too, express our love for God by inviting God *as* Love and Mercy into our life. And we, too, love God by allowing Love to embrace us and to become our self-acceptance and self-love; by allowing the Holy Spirit of God's Love to pray in us and to become our prayer to God; and by allowing Love to flow through us to others and to become our charity toward others, allowing us in charity, at the very least, to be nonviolent and make no enemies.

St. Thérèse of Lisieux read the parable of the Pharisee and the publican as an invitation to be totally available to God in the whole truth of who she was with her gifts and blessings, her weakness and sinfulness. The parable became one of her favorite stories in Scripture. She recognized that Jesus was portraying two distinct ways that we attempt to come prayerfully to God to be freed, redeemed, and united with God. The Pharisee's way is the false path of rejecting that our goodness comes from God and willfully striving to establish our goodness on the basis of our own virtues and good works. That path subordinates our relationship to God to a deception, to a legality founded on our response to our obligations and to the law. It is a relationship devoid of love.

The publican's way, on the contrary, is the gospel path of loving God by being willingly available to God's love in a relationship of reciprocity. This path acknowledges that all good in us is from God's mercy and subordinates virtues, good works, and achievements to our loving relationship to God. This path welcomes God's love into us and extends God's love to others in charity. It elevates truth and humility as the highest spiritual priorities. It positions us to rejoice in God's love and share it with others. The publican's way of loving God by welcoming God's love is presented by Jesus as the authentic gospel way of holiness.

Thérèse, at the end of her life, wrote that she would go to God, not by the way of the Pharisee, but simply by sharing in the prayer of the publican.[1] The publican's prayerful way of being authentically available to God in the reality of who he was is the path that Thérèse has reaffirmed as the gospel way of holiness and has given to the church as her "little way."

"Lord, be merciful to me, a sinner." This prayer from a heart honest, humble, and contrite, which unites us with the legions of faithful "little ones" who, over the centuries of Christianity, have prayed it as the Jesus prayer, is the prayer Jesus asks of us. And this prayerful way is enough. The publican "goes down justified."

1. *Story of a Soul: The Autobiography of St. Thérèse of Lisieux*, 3rd ed., trans. John Clarke (Washington, DC: ICS Publications, 1996), 258.

11 . Presence and Absence

Remembering That We Are in the Presence of God

We are at all times and in all places in the presence of God, because God "is not far from any of us, since it is in [God] that we live, and move, and exist" (Acts 17:27-28, NJB). God is always present to us, loving us into being, but we are not always present to God. We sometimes absent ourselves from God's presence. We neglect practices that remind us that we are in the presence of God, and we sometimes even engage in practices that take us away from remembering. But remembering that we are in the presence of God is one of the most important acts of mindfulness that we can cultivate in our practice of praying our experiences.

To remember that we are in the presence of God does not primarily mean to affirm a theological doctrine; nor does it mean in the first instance to think devout thoughts about God. Rather, to remember that we are in the presence of God is to be as aware and appreciative as we can be of the reality of our life story, and to offer ourselves to God in our story in a spirit of surrender and gratitude, allowing our story to be enfolded into God's story.

To remember that we are in the presence of God is not an intellectual feat but a moment of mindfulness, a moment of personal self-awareness, a moment of integration and personal honesty. It is also a moment of self-appropriation and self-appreciation. It is a moment of complete self-surrender and gratitude that encompasses our relationship to God, to ourselves, to others, and to all of creation. It is primarily a moment of being swept up in the loving arms of God and, therefore, a moment of self-transcendence. It is a moment of coming home to our true self.

To remember that we are in the presence of God is to explicitly remember that we and all of creation are in the presence of Love, that all of creation and our own deepest reality participate in Love, that we are loved, and that we are called to live in Love, die in Love, and live again in Love.

But even with our best intentions, our interest in remembering that we are in the presence of God seems to flag, perhaps at times even to fail us. Our mindfulness diminishes, our prayer fades, and sometimes only in retrospect do we have a sense of having been absent from the loving reality of the always-present God. This sense of being absent from God often manifests itself either in our being absent *from* prayer or our being absent *during* prayer.

We sometimes experience ourselves being absent *from* prayer when we find that excessive hours spent at work or in other responsibilities or activities fill our days and leave little formal time for prayer. It is true that excessive work and involvements may make us absent from times of prayer, but work and involvements do not automatically make us absent from prayerfulness; they do not necessarily make us absent from God. They make us absent from God only if they are the kinds of involvements that feed self-centeredness and self-promotion and ultimately nourish the false self. They make us absent from God if they flow from the same attitude that took the Pharisee into the temple to pray.

It is possible, therefore, that we can be involved in many responsibilities and work long hours with little formal time for prayer, and yet be involved prayerfully, mindfully in what we are doing. That is, we can be involved in our duties and activities in such a way that we carry with us in our daily life and work the attitude of the publican, implicitly mindful of our weakness and implicitly invoking God's mercy. Then our work and involvements would not be self-centered and would not be opportunities for feeding the false self.

We are absent *from* prayer, therefore, not necessarily when we are involved in many things, but only when those many things feed our selfishness without concern for God. We are absent *from* prayer, then, when perhaps we would rather not be with God or pray our experiences. Perhaps we are indifferent to the reality of God's presence. Or perhaps we resist the awareness of God's presence because that remembrance might awaken in us distressing feelings; it might challenge us into ways we would rather not go. We might resist being present to God because, at this time, we are not ready to face in his presence that part of ourself that we know is our false self. So we mistakenly tell ourselves, "I cannot really pray unless I clear up the garbage in my life and get beyond my defenses. Unless I do this, I will not get in touch with the center of my life where God dwells. I need first to do something with the parts of my life that I have tried to ignore—my excessive bitterness, my hostility, my violence to myself and others, my coldness, my emptiness." This is the way we sometimes talk to ourselves, rationalizing our being absent *from* God, but it is a mistaken way.

We are ashamed of our false self, and we see the presence of God as a mirror or a light that illumines our false self with all its weaknesses and deceptions as it struggles for control of our heart. We are afraid or hurt or hostile, and our solution is to divert our attention from God. We do not want to bring our experiences into the presence of God until we are more honorable and presentable. "I'll pray when I get over this disturbing situation," we mistakenly tell ourselves. We want to be like the Pharisee and tell God about our righteousness. We might identify with those who falsely believe, "I can't pray because of my personal weaknesses. I could say I love and adore God in a prayer from a book, but my actions during the day contradict what I say. And so, I stop praying." This way is a mistake.

In our weakness, we are embarrassed or afraid to take time to be available to God, and so our excessive involvement is a way of avoiding prayer. But by absenting ourself *from* prayer, we are only compounding our problem, because God welcomes us specifically in our sinfulness and distress. The path of the publican is the gospel path, but we fail to take it. Instead of taking time to pray those very experiences that distress and embarrass us, we fill our life with diversions, with extra work, with excitements and thrills. We go shopping again, or do a bit more work, or search the Internet a while longer, or continue aimless reading, or move into other forms of distraction and addiction. In short, we fill our life with trash. We simply resist for weeks or months consciously and explicitly praying especially our disturbing experiences. We may still take some time for church, and no one may notice, but we know that our life is drifting.

Then it seems that the excessive work and the many involvements are merely symptoms of the real problem. The real problem is our misdirected heart, the false self feeding on the fear and embarrassment, being nourished by the perfectionistic nonsense and power struggles in our life. The excessive work and involvements that leave little time for prayer simply allow us to keep moving in life, and permit us to appear as if we were living. But we are dead inside. Our true self is crying out to be with God, but by being absent from prayerfulness, we are absent from God.

We are absent *during* prayer when we are distracted from an awareness of the presence of God during a time when we more consciously wish to be aware of God's presence in personal prayer. Distractions *during* prayer are wanderings of our mind or tricks of our imagination or eruptions of our feelings that take our attention away from the topic or focus of the prayer. If we are using a book of prayers, they distract us from the prayer we are reading. If we are meditating on the Scriptures, they distract us from the content of the passage. If we are praying with devotions or aspirations of our heart or if we are attempting to be centered or available to God in simple attention to God's love, they divert our focus to something else.

These wanderings and images are nuisances, because they distract us from our predetermined expectations of what our prayer time should be. But they need not separate or distract us from God. They may not be the context in which we wish to be present to God, but they may, in fact, be the context in which God wishes to be present to us. In that sense, our "distractions" may be invitations to explore in faith the truth of our experiences to which these "distractions" point.

We need to consider that perhaps we are invited and challenged to make our "distractions" *during* prayer the new *content* of our prayer, letting them lead us into a part of our life that we may not have seen clearly before. In that way, our joys and delights as well as our anger, our bitterness, our violent thoughts and feelings, our awareness of our weakness and faults, our memory of past experiences that we have tucked away and wished we did not have—all of these may surface and become the ways in which God wants to be present to us. In this way, the Holy Spirit may be wishing to pray in us. In this way, even our so-called "distractions" can become part of our prayer.

On one occasion, St. Thérèse was asked what she did when, during her private prayer time, her mind was filled with distractions. She responded, "I have a lot of these, but as soon as I perceive them I pray for the persons that occupy my imagination and this way they benefit from my distractions."[1]

By praying for those persons who were "distractions" in her prayer, her "distractions" became her prayer. But St. Thérèse also prayed her "distractions" by accepting and appreciating her diversions from prayer—and even her falling asleep during prayer—as graces to acknowledge her weakness. She turned her weakness into prayer by honestly accepting the limitations in herself. Her prayer, then, became another opportunity to see herself as the publican asking for God's mercy.

The real distractions *during* prayer, the way we are absent from God even during times we put aside for personal prayer, are when we accommodate and nurture the movements within us that take us from the presence of who we really are in God's hands. Then we involve ourselves with the demands of the false self. These demands are our need to be self-centered, self-indulgent, self-deceptive, or self-protective, as was the Pharisee. We move into concerns and images that feed our need to be right and perfect, powerful, secure, and praised. These are the daydreams of personal victories and ego-centered plans for personal security and success. They were the real obstacles to the Pharisee's prayer.

We also absent ourself from the presence of God *during* prayer when we justify past mistakes, and thus negate God's call to constant conversion. We sometimes reconstruct memories in a self-justifying way, thereby distorting our story in such a way that we, and not God, are at the center of our life. Prompted by the false self, these real distractions trap us into self-promotion or self-pity. They ensnare us in attachments to our feeling good about ourself.

Our absence from the presence of God *during* prayer can also be more subtle. We may absent ourself from our life in God by devotional thoughts that are not our own and that take us from the truth of our story. We might use thoughts and prayers from pious books, for example, as a way to avoid reflecting on the issues of our own life that we need to bring into the presence of God. Or our false self might even use the words of formal prayer to protect itself from being honest before God, and yet allow us to fill the time we devote to prayer. Thus, we might "pray" like the Pharisee. These tendencies are a distraction from the presence of God, because they absent us from the reality that we are in God's hands. They lure us away from the truth about ourselves that unites us to God.

Our tendency to absent ourself *from* prayer or *during* prayer tells us that the false self is still powerful in our life. Its lingering influence helps us to know that praying our experiences is a life-long process. It is also a call to patience, confident that our life is in God's hands and that our transformation is in God's time.

The distress we feel when, in retrospect, we become aware that we have absented ourself *from* prayer or *during* prayer and have neglected to "remember we are in the presence of God" may seem to be yet another "negative" experience, another victory of our false self. But that sense of distress is itself an indication that the Spirit of Truth calls us unceasingly. We would not be aware of our reluctance to pray our experiences unless we were moved by that Spirit of Truth. Our false self is exposed by the Spirit of Truth gently, compassionately, relentlessly. And nowhere do we experience our false self more forcefully than in our capacity to be absent from God, who at every present moment is loving us, nevertheless, into being who we really are.

1. Sr. Geneviève of the Holy Face (Céline Martin), *My Sister St. Thérèse* (Rockford, IL: Tan Books and Publishers, Inc., 1997), 25.

12. MINISTRY

Good Works, Prayer, and Ambiguity

St. John Baptist de La Salle, founder of the apostolic congregation of Brothers of the Christian Schools and himself considerably gifted in prayer, emphasized the value of doing good works as an expression of prayer and faith and as a means of spiritual growth. He, of course, encouraged the brothers of his community to take formal time for prayer, and he composed a book of meditations for their reflection. He was, however, realistic enough to know that since they worked in the ministry of education, the brothers would sometimes be interrupted in their time of spiritual devotions and prayer for the sake of serving their students. He told the brothers that when these interruptions became necessary, they should accept the call to service as a kind of prayer itself. What was important was that the brothers—whether they were doing good works or were at prayer—be motivated by their desire to do the will of God. Their good works done with the intention of pleasing God were not to be distinguished from their formal times of prayer, but both were to be done in a spirit of faith and zeal.

De La Salle also knew that even during the formal times of prayer, the brothers would often be preoccupied with their daily teaching activities, their thoughts directed toward solving the problems that filled their ministry. He understood, moreover, that this preoccupation need not be a distraction but could serve as the content of their prayer.

De La Salle directed his brothers to incorporate reflection about their ministry into their meditation, even when they were on retreat. In his *Meditations for the Time of Retreat*, he remarked, "You must constantly represent the needs of your [students] to Jesus Christ, explaining to him the difficulties you experience in guiding them."[1] De La Salle would certainly have his brothers pray for their students, asking God to bless them and to give them the graces to avoid sin. But, further, he would have his brothers specifically and consciously reflect, as a form of prayer, on their own work in the schools. He recommended that the brothers speak to the Lord, for instance, about their recurring difficulties in correcting their students.

A brother's memories of his angry reaction to a problem student, or his feelings of appreciation at the success of his students, or his feelings of weakness and conflict as he tried to correct a student, or the pain of his attempts at reconciliation, or the indecisiveness of his efforts to divert a student from selfishness—these memories and feelings were to be laid out and explained to the Lord as the content of the brother's prayer. The brother's prayer, therefore, might consist of unfolding these memories and feelings to bring him to a deeper self-knowledge of his motives, his values, his weaknesses, his power of love, and his force of hate and violence.

In his directives, De La Salle constantly returned to the need for the brothers to integrate their work and their prayer, and praying their experiences was one of the ways De La Salle understood that this integration would take place. It was also one of the ways he believed the brothers would come to self-knowledge and come to understand and purify their motives.

De La Salle warned, as have all those wise in the spiritual life, that we ought to be cautious of our best intentions. Yet this caution should not block our engagement in good works. It would be unreal to engage only in works that we thought were motivated solely by perfect intentions. No such thing is humanly possible. We are called to be as aware as possible of our motivations, to move as far from selfishness and self-centeredness as possible, and then to do the best we can at any given moment. Personal awareness, sensitivity to our weaknesses, honesty, personal reflection, and prayer are indispensable in this process. Those who in retrospect reflect seriously on their good works often come to a self-knowledge that exposes the ambiguity of their motivations.

De La Salle recommends to those in ministry,

Examine before God how you are acting in your ministry and whether you are failing in any of your responsibilities. Come to know yourself just as you are. Find fault with yourself accurately, unsparingly, so that when Jesus Christ comes to judge you, you will be able to face his judgment without being afraid.[2]

We come to know ourselves just as we are when we reflect with honesty and openness on our experiences. To "examine before God how you are acting" is to enter the path of praying your experiences. It is a different way of saying what Teresa of Ávila said about being sustained by the bread of the awareness of one's sins.

St. Thérèse of Lisieux, who must also be numbered among those wise in the spiritual life, was a leader among her own sisters in her Carmelite community. Thérèse was asked to direct the newer members of the community along the spiritual path, and she, like De La Salle, emphasized the importance of self-knowledge and awareness of feelings and motives.

Once, when still a novice, Thérèse took aside a young sister to warn the sister privately and discreetly of her ambiguous motives. The young sister was unaware that she had a crush on the mother superior. Thérèse had personally experienced this same feeling, and so she could warn the young sister of motives and feelings the sister herself was not completely conscious of. The sister's love of the superior was motivated not solely by her goodwill but more by her desire to be noticed and appreciated by the superior. The young sister's love was really a subtle form of selfishness. The young sister, supported by Thérèse's concern and honesty, came to her own humble acknowledgment of her ambiguous motivation.

Thérèse encouraged the younger sisters for whom she was responsible to examine their motives and to be aware, not only of their gifts, but also of their failings and weaknesses. Regarding personal faults, Thérèse had two pieces of advice that she had learned from praying her own experiences. She suggested that when the young sisters noticed their faults, they do what she did: "I entrust to Jesus my failings; I tell Him all about them; and I think, so bold is my trust, that in this way I acquire more power over His heart and draw to myself in still grater abundance the love of Him who came to call sinners, not the righteous."[3] It was a way of turning the recognition of personal inadequacy and failure into prayer.

The second bit of advice Thérèse also shared from her own experience. She advised her sisters not to become violently self-critical but rather to forgive themselves when they failed at their responsibilities or when they became aware of having ambiguous motives. She offered some of her best spiritual advice to a sister who was discouraged by her own continuing failings and weaknesses. The young sister was putting herself down, and Thérèse encouraged her with these words of wisdom: "If you are willing to bear serenely the trial of being displeasing to yourself, then you will be . . . [for Jesus] a pleasant place of shelter."[4] Being patient with ourselves, forgiving ourselves, and properly loving ourselves, Thérèse suggested, were important ways to allow God to love us even in our failures. To become discouraged with ourselves when we failed was to be violent to ourselves, and Thérèse recognized that that was not the gospel way.

When we were young, we might have felt that we could easily overcome our faults and do good works for God. Being virtuous, doing good works, and even loving others were, we might have imagined, only a matter of training, strategy, and good intentions. Now that we are older, we may be aware that we sometimes have had selfish motives in our love and that there may be some truth in G. K. Chesterton's quip that perhaps most of our virtue is simply a lack of opportunity. We may certainly be more aware that most of our good works have been done at least in part for ourselves.

To gain status among our colleagues, to exert power over those with whom we were working, to express a talent for organization in our specialty—these might have been part of the motivations that have produced our successful project.

In our successes, we may receive genuine appreciation from the people with whom we work. They may say a word of thanks for the good we have done for them, or they may tell us how much our friendship has meant to them. We rightly acknowledge the good in ourselves, yet often we are also rightly uneasy with the praise of others. We feel that our efforts have not been great enough to warrant such gratitude. We know that our motivation has often been tinged with selfishness. In praying these experiences, we become aware that the power going out from us to effect good in others originates well beyond ourselves. We begin to appreciate the power of the Holy Spirit that we now sense operating through us. Our effectiveness, our patience, our gentleness, our understanding—all of "our" goodness has been given to us and used by the God beyond us.

People have praised us for our good works, and we cannot deny that our works have helped others to live more human and faithful lives. On the one hand, we cannot reject as evil our desire to develop our own talents or to express our power of efficiency and organization. On the other hand, we know the ambiguity of our motivations, and we know that any good we have done is really God's work through us.

Even our growth in faith and trust has been a gift. No amount of our own cleverness has produced it. As we grow in self-knowledge, we begin to experience God's blessings—until we at last realize that all of life is a gift. The goodness of the Spirit has used our good will, and we feel ourselves drawn to offer prayerful thanks to God for our willingness to be an instrument in God's hands.

As we come to know ourselves as we are, we are invited "to recognize one's nothingness and to abandon oneself as a child into God's arms," as St. Thérèse reminded us.[5] In such abandonment, we "will be able to face his judgment without being afraid," as De La Salle advised his brothers.

Sometimes involvement in ministry is experienced as an obstacle to prayer. Times of involvement in good works may seem to take us away from times of prayer. But this dichotomy will not be the case when our involvement in doing good works becomes the very content of our prayer. As we pray our experiences of ministry, we resolve the conflict we may feel between works and prayer. Our ministry ceases to be a distraction to prayer. It becomes, rather, through self-knowledge, the nourishment of prayer as well as the expression of prayer and faith. Our prayer becomes the vessel for holding our self and our works before God in humility and gratitude. We more easily establish a balance between our time of personal prayer and our involvements. As we pray our experiences of work and ministry, and as our life becomes the focus of our prayer offering to God, the tension between prayer and work begins to dissolve.

1. John Baptiste de La Salle, *Meditations for the Time of Retreat* (Romeoville, IL: Christian Brothers Conference, 1975), 56.

2. De La Salle, 89.

3. Ida Friederike Görres, *The Hidden Face: A Study of St. Thérèse of Lisieux* (San Francisco: Ignatius Press, 2003), 337.

4. *Collected Letters of Saint Thérèse of Lisieux,* trans. F. J. Sheed, 303; cf. *General Correspondence: Letters of St. Thérèse of Lisieux,* vol. 2, trans. John Clarke (Washington, DC: ICS Publications, 1982, 1988), 1038, for a slightly different translation.

5. *General Correspondence,* vol. 2, 1094.

13. FAITH

Incarnation and Truth

Carl Jung is reported to have remarked that the greatest mistake of religious people was that they allowed their faith to preclude or filter their experiences. Jung was rightly rejecting a narrow view of faith. For some people, faith does preclude experience, and we have seen that for others, the Scriptures can have the same effect. Indeed, we should be suspicious of anything—even an understanding of faith or the Scriptures or prayer—that suggests that we devalue the concrete, everyday realities in our life. Incarnational faith, which is Christian faith, proclaims that in our unique and personal story, God is lovingly active.

If faith involved nothing more than assenting to particular doctrines, then faith would tend to distort, filter, and negate experience. If faith meant that certain doctrines were to be held as truth even in the face of developing knowledge and growing experience, then faith would indeed be the negative force Jung rejected. But if we more rightly understand that by faith we do not so much hold truths as Truth—God's Truth—holds us, then faith calls us into our experiences and is a way of being present to our experiences, a way of entering into their depths with trust and thanksgiving. Faith calls us, not to preclude our experiences, but to include them, to enfold them into God's story. For, it is through praying our experiences that we engage and express our faith, that we discover the truth of ourself in relation to God.

We are called to search out in our ordinary and confusing personal and communal story the truth that we glibly affirm in theory: that God's life flows into our life. In particular, we are called to become aware that we are weak and sinful, limited and broken, yet blessed and graced and gifted. We are called to "recognize one's nothingness and to abandon oneself as a child into God's arms," as St. Thérèse of Lisieux tells us.[1] Our life story is the clay out of which this realization is fashioned. We are called to take our personal story seriously. The joys and struggles, the care and hurt (both given and received), are all testimonies from our everyday life that God is in our life and that we can entrust ourselves to his presence. We are invited to unfold these experiences and to let God's loving presence come through for our praise and gratitude.

Sometimes an experience may startle us into an awareness of brokenness or blessedness. The death of a friend brings us to a realization of the preciousness of love and the beauty of friendship. This realization is an experience of faith.

We are also brought up short by an awareness of how shot through with selfishness our love for others has sometimes been. We recall the many acts of petty jealousy and the missed occasions when an affirmation or word of intimacy would have healed. We experience now in this pettiness and weakness a sure sign of our sinfulness, for all those acts of selfishness are surely acts of resistance to grace. This realization is an experience of faith.

We know that our self-centeredness could even take us into the darkness of rejoicing in the suffering of our dearest friend. We experience, too, in the death of one we struggled to love, our own mortality and the pressing weight of our own death. These realizations strike with clarity and force. When they come upon us, we become aware that God is judging and enlightening us in our weakness, calling and empowering us to deeper integrity. All of this is also an experience of faith.

A moment of beauty and joy or a moment of intimacy may put us in touch with an awareness of God's love and blessing. We ride on a mountain road, or walk along a beach, or experience the affection and complete acceptance of a friend, and we are suddenly awake to the realization that at work in our life is a force of love and care that fully encompasses us and all of reality. We see more clearly that we are loved quite undeservedly, not just by a friend, but by Life. We become more aware that we and all of creation are being sustained and nourished by a beneficent free Love. And in this, we encounter God's word uttered in blessing and care. This also is an experience of faith.

We could call experiences of such clarity and force "religious experiences" or "faith experiences" and then refer to other more ordinary experiences as "secular experiences." But this kind of distinction does not hold up. The experiences of God's presence through the form of judgment or love may come upon us most vividly in unique moments that are themselves gifts, but God's word and presence are also available in the depths of all our experiences. We would be closer to the truth to speak of the "religious or faith dimension" of every experience.

God is addressing us in all moments of life. We may experience some moments as more privileged than others because they reveal with more clarity and force our limitations and our giftedness.

That this revelatory power is more apparent in some moments than others is due more to our own openness and readiness than to the intensity and availability of God's saving presence.

St. Teresa of Ávila, too, referred to experience as revelatory of God's word. "Experience is a great help in all," she wrote in her autobiography, "for it teaches what is suitable for us; and God can be served in everything."[2] St. Thérèse of Lisieux made the point more succinctly, following the teaching of St. Paul, when she said, "Everything is grace."[3]

Our task, then, is to become aware of those obstacles of egoism that block the truth of our experiences and to allow those obstacles to be purged by the Spirit of Truth. Our faith calls us to search our experiences, to preclude none of them, to relish all of them, trying to reach that limit, that depth, where the sound of God's word of judgment and grace will become clear.

1. *General Correspondence: Letters of St. Thérèse of Lisieux,* vol. 2, trans. John Clarke (Washington, DC: ICS Publications, 1982, 1988), 1094.

2. *The Book of Her Life,* in *The Collected Works of St. Teresa of Ávila,* trans. Kieran Kavanaugh and Otilio Rodriguez (Washington, DC: ICS Publications, 1976), 83.

3. *St. Thérèse of Lisieux: Her Last Conversations,* trans. John Clarke (Washington, DC: ICS Publications, 1977), 57.

14. Healing Hurtful Memories

Acknowledging, Accepting, and Appreciating

All our experiences possess a revelatory power, yet we find ourselves unable to reflect on some of them. They are too disconcerting. They are too hurtful. We do not want to resurrect the pain of the argument with a friend, which ruptured a budding and precious relationship. We do not want ever again to feel the sense of rejection and loneliness that the memory of our relationship with our father or mother may bring. We resist reminders of our jealousy or our sensuality that have led us into spiteful and selfish acts. We do not want to think about our failure as a young teacher or our blunders in our first years of marriage. We do not want to reopen wounds that have scarred over.

When we label these painful experiences "wounds," we must remember that this is *our* label. We say that they are injuries to our sensitivities, to our expectations, to our hopes, to our sense of propriety and dignity and success; but, as they manifest a part of the truth about ourselves, they are not wounds but facets of the precious totality of our life. Our prayer will be hindered to the extent that we cannot gather up all of the reality of our life into our offering to God.

Prayer is fundamentally an offering of ourselves to God. It is not a matter of presenting to God the pious thoughts of theologians or spiritual writers, or simply the pious prayers in books. Nor is it a matter of offering to God only what we believe to be worthy of the Creator—our successes, our virtues, our goodness—as if they were our achievements to be given with a dignified obeisance. We offer to God who we are now: all of those longings for the Lord and all of those egotistical schemes that form part of our desires.

All of this is part of us, and this is all we have to offer to God.

The parts of ourselves left out of our offering weaken our gift. God wants all of us, and so we work toward an integration of all of our memories and hopes into our total gift. To achieve this integrity requires that in some way the memories that cause pain and resistance must be healed.

When we refer to the healing of memories, we are not speaking about morbidly dragging up hurtful experiences that have already settled. We are speaking of those painful experiences that are still with us and cry out for our attention. These memories come to us often by surprise. They recur when we least expect them. We do not drag them up; they come to our awareness of their own power because they have more to say to us. They are the memories that, like festering wounds, tell us they need our attention. Only by acknowledging, accepting, and finally, appreciating our painful experiences can we make them part of our complete offering of ourselves to the Lord.

In *acknowledging* our painful experiences as part of our personal story, we begin to open ourselves to the possibility of being nourished by God through those experiences. To the extent that we deny an experience, however hurtful, we deny God's loving care, which is mysteriously embedded in that experience.

Sometimes we may fear that if we even acknowledge a painful experience, it will gain control over us. We falsely imagine that if we simply never think of it again, it will go away. This, of course, does not happen.

If an experience causes pain and disturbance when it comes to mind, we can be certain that it is disturbing us even when we are not aware of it. Casting an experience out of our memory does not cast its power out of our life. By not acknowledging and accepting these painful memories, we permit them to have power over us. We become bound by that part of our past. We are not free in relationship to it. We are defensive toward it, and we cannot be nourished by it.

This lack of freedom is also an indication of a blockage in our prayer. We have not yet gathered together all of ourselves in our offering to the Lord.

We don't free ourselves by rejecting the past as something "I'll never think of again"; rather, we free ourselves when we integrate our past into our total life story. The offering of ourselves to the Lord, then, approaches a completeness.

By ignoring painful experiences, we allow them to control us in a profound and subtle way. By acknowledging them, we begin to reduce their control and begin to establish a relationship with them that eliminates the feeling of our being victimized by them. A helpful example of this is the notion of "naming" in the Scriptures. God required Adam to name the animals before Adam could have "dominion over them"—a dominion, not of overpowering, but a relationship in which Adam was neither fearful nor oppressive. This was a sign that Adam's relationship to the animals was one of freedom and appropriate control (see Genesis 2:19-20). When Jesus wished to establish a deeper, proper relationship with Peter, Jesus named Peter (see Matthew 16:17-19). For us, too, naming an experience helps us to form the proper relationship with it, not by overpowering it or doing violence to it, but by integrating it into our life as Adam accepted the animals into his world and as Jesus accepted Peter as a leader in the church.

In acknowledging and naming a painful experience, we begin the process of healing, because we begin the process of living the truth. This truth, Jesus assures us, will set us free, because it is enfolded in that most ultimate of truths: God's love. The process of healing of memories is primarily a process of letting the whole truth of our personal story be enfolded in the all-encompassing truth of God's love.

By our simple acknowledgment, we take the first step toward healing the pain of the memory. The second step is to broaden that acknowledgment into an attitude of *acceptance*, admitting both the experience and the pain as a part of ourselves.

At this point, not only have we recognized that a painful experience does exist in our life, but we have begun to accept it as a significant one. We now begin to realize that by its recurrence in memory and by the intensity of the related pain, the experience is asking to be brought to a reconciliation.

This reconciliation begins when our relationship with the event shifts from that of an adversarial, violent (over-against) relationship to that of a welcoming, dialogical (one-with) relationship. This shift indicates that we have come to a level of reverence and respect for the experience, realizing that it will speak truth to us. Prayer has often been described as listening to God; we may hear God if we open ourselves to hear what our painful experience has to say.

God speaks to us when we allow our personal life to address us as we open ourselves in a listening attitude in the quiet that follows our questions: "What does this experience have to say about my way of living, my way of relating to others? . . . What does this experience have to say about my priorities in life? What is the cause of the hurt? . . .What are the feelings that surround the hurt, and did these feelings originally arise, perhaps, in childhood in my life? What would be required of me for the experience to no longer be hurtful? . . . What does all of this say about my ability to abandon myself 'as a child into God's arms'?"

Further, moving from acknowledging a painful experience to accepting it with reverence often calls for forgiveness. Frequently the pain itself is founded in our lack of forgiveness: we have not forgiven ourselves, and we have not forgiven others; perhaps we have not forgiven God.

Perhaps the painful experience shows us our weakness or sinfulness. Perhaps our stupidity or sloth or self-centeredness motivated us to a foolish action we now sincerely regret. The memory brings with it a deep awareness of the sinfulness that is still with us. At times, we cannot believe that the Lord has already forgiven us, and we forget that Jesus asks us to forgive ourselves.

Perhaps the painful experience was caused by the cruelty of others or by their insensitivity or their hatred toward us. Whether the problem lasted several minutes or several years, we are now called to forgive the other and to move our attention from clutching the hostile feelings flowing from the hurt to a deeper awareness of the loving presence of God. We are asked to accept the reality that the God who loves both us and the other is offering us this memory as a way of getting closer to Jesus.

Forgiveness of ourselves and others does not require a rational justification; indeed, forgiving is often not a "reasonable" act. Forgiveness is first of all an act of faith. It requires faith in the power of God's love to bring good out of evil. This faith will not be achieved merely by our rethinking the experience. Our experience, as we suggested, is like a koan, and thus our thought and reason fail us, because God's forgiveness and power are not encompassed by reason. Rather, our faith is enkindled in the quiet of imagining Jesus moving toward us, accepting us and others as he accepted Zacchaeus and the adulterous woman (see Luke 19:1-10; John 7:53–8:11). In our imagination, we can experience what our thoughts and reason fail to comprehend. Abandoning and going beyond reason, we can experience the warmth of the arms of our loving God.

Forgiveness of ourselves and others allows us to accept more fully the memory of the experience as a part of ourselves. We can now more completely incorporate the event as a part of our offering to the Lord. We now also begin to realize that the painful experience is a source of growth, because it invites us to accept both our weakness and God's love.

The final step in the healing of painful memories that follows from acknowledgment and acceptance is *appreciation*. Memories are healed and our prayer is complete when we come full circle and appreciate our painful experience. We reverently take up that hard rock of experience rejected by the builders within ourselves and accept it as the cornerstone of a new stage of growth.

We say yes, a grateful yes, to all that has been. We embrace our experience as a little death leading to a little resurrection. We appreciate even our most painful experiences, realizing that all things can work for good for those who love God (see Romans 8:28; Philippians 1:6).

Redemptive suffering is most likely to be found, not in the suffering of the body or in some romanticized oppression, but in the profound sadness of knowing the truth about our pettiness, self-pity, and vulnerability, as well as our violence to ourselves and others. Thérèse of Lisieux remarked, "To suffer our imperfections with patience, this is true sanctity."[1] This is also the awareness of St. Paul when he prayed, "If I must boast, I will boast of the things that show my weakness" (2 Corinthians 11:30).

In the process of healing our memories we include in our treasury of self-giving to the Lord all of our experiences, especially those that have spoken to us so vividly of our vulnerability and sinfulness. And we offer these painful experiences to God as our prayerful participation in the paschal mystery, in which death is swallowed up in victory (see 1 Corinthians 15:54).

We know a memory has been healed when it speaks to us no longer of pain or brokenness or of any form of violence to ourselves or others, but rather reveals God's mercy and love. The memory has been healed when we can say what St. Thérèse said about the pain that her faults caused her: "The memory of my faults humbles me; it causes me never to rely on my own strength, which is but weakness, but especially it teaches me a further lesson of the mercy and love of God."[2]

When we pray our experiences, we are willing to acknowledge, name, accept, forgive, integrate, and appreciate all of our personal story so that our prayer of offering might be complete. In the process, we heal our memories, because now those painful memories speak to us more of God's love than of our hurt.

1. *General Correspondence: Letters of St. Thérèse of Lisieux,* vol. 2, trans. John Clarke (Washington, DC: ICS Publications, 1982, 1988), 1122.

2. *General Correspondence,* 1133.

15. OUR BEST PRAYER

Our Own Prayer

Claire was never very good at sports, but like the other students at her high school, she had to have a certain number of credits in physical education to graduate. Junior year—the year that the girls played basketball—was about to start, and Claire dreaded the thought of humiliating herself in yet another sport.

Fortunately for Claire, the school gym was being renovated that year, and the physical education class had to be held in an ordinary classroom. So thirty-five girls sat in rows of desks, some taking notes, some just with their hands folded, as the teacher taught them basketball. The teacher wrote on the board the definition of a dribble, a hook shot, and a fade-away jumper and detailed the advantages of a fast break and a box defense. The girls listened attentively. They even read from the biographies of some basketball stars. Claire didn't touch a basketball all year— she didn't even see a game—but she got an A in basketball.

There is much these days to help us learn about prayer. There are many books about prayer and about those in the Christian tradition who have been noted for their prayer. There are lectures, workshops, retreats, and academic courses on prayer. And much stress is placed today on "techniques" of prayer: bodily postures, breathing exercises, and sequences of thoughts or images, which are offered to help us with prayer. All of these may indeed be helpful; they may be informative and inspiring, but at some point we get the feeling that we are sitting at a desk listening, instead of being on the basketball court playing the game.

Wanting to know *about* prayer for the sake of intellectual interest, curiosity about how other people pray, or searching out information about techniques of prayer is like wanting to know *about* friendship or love. There is much to know about friendship and love, things that we can find inspiring in the lives of people who develop friendships or who love faithfully and well. We could attend workshops on interpersonal communication, for example, and read books on the topic, but all of this is quite different from actually loving faithfully or being a good friend.

The real issue about love and friendship is not whether we have studied enough academically or whether we know all the techniques, but rather who we are as loving persons and who we are called to be. All the techniques for love and friendship that we know in advance must be subsumed into our personal, unique ways of loving and being a good friend that we know only in retrospect. Similarly, there are no infallible techniques of prayer that will lead to a deeper relationship with God; there is only the longing of the heart to follow.

If we want to deepen our relationship with God, we must be in touch with our heart, in which the Spirit of Love already resides and empowers us. And similar to our experience of trying to love a human being, our prayer is a personal, unique, and above all, creative experience that unfolds as we come to know ourselves in the presence of God.

There are ways of personal prayer that have developed over centuries and that we come to know by studying the tradition of prayer. But these ways are intended to inspire us and not to replace the way of prayer that comes to us as we actually pray. To come to know our unique way of prayer is not to disregard the tradition but to respond to the tradition. One of the wisest bits of traditional advice about prayer is simply this: "Pray the way you can and not the way you can't." Sometimes studying prayer as a subject leads us to want to pray the way that is recommended by a teacher or a book. True, we can be informed and even inspired by others, but our prayer is fundamentally unique and can only become known to us as we truly seek God.

An American young man went to India in search of God. In his quest for spiritual growth. he came under the guidance of a famous guru. The young man lived with the guru for a number of weeks, and one day while the two were out walking beside a quiet lake, the young man found courage to ask the question, "How do I find God?" The guru looked at the young man in astonishment and said, "There are no methods to finding God; follow your heart."

The young man insisted that there must be techniques, short-cuts, practices. The guru shook his head and then suddenly jumped on the young man, catching him quite off balance, then threw him to the ground, dragged him to the edge of the lake, and thrust his head under the water. The young man was shocked when he sensed that he was being held under the water by a strong and determined set of hands and was, in truth, drowning. He struggled, but to no avail. He grew panicky and lunged with all his might, until he finally managed to get his head out of the water and crawl away, exhausted.

Shocked and still gasping for breath, the young man screamed at the guru, "You tried to drown me!" The guru replied, "When you seek union with God with the same intensity that you are gasping for air, then you will find God." There are no techniques for finding God, for deepening prayer; accomplishing this is a matter of making it the desire of our life and then allowing ourselves to be led, to become ourselves a prayer.

All of this implies that our prayer will develop as we strive to be honest with ourselves about who we are in the presence of God. As we share with God what at any given moment we know to be our truth, we are really participating in the movement of the Spirit of Truth already praying within us. And that is our best prayer.

Some will recognize that praying our experiences is a method of prayer that they have used off and on for many years. These persons may not be able to articulate why reflecting on their experiences felt like prayer, but they know it has been a source of the strength, enlightenment, transformation, growth, and peace that have traditionally been associated with prayer. They also know that in this process they have been in the presence of the Lord of their life and they have been challenged to deeper intimacy with God.

These persons may find encouragement in continuing to pray their experiences. They may also begin to notice sources other than the Scriptures or formal religious exercises impelling them into the depths of their experiences.

Our life, we profess, is lived in God. There is no doubt that we can find God in the depths and flow of our own experiences. On occasion we will have to take formal, personal time for this kind of reflection, but ultimately it is in the very process of living our daily existence that we are called to find God's word and to offer ourselves in response. When we purify our stance toward life so that our self-centeredness is out of the way, and when openness and reverence are at the center of our life, then we will find one experience clarifying another, and all of our life revealing the caring presence of God and leading us to self-offering.

The greatest gift that we are asked to accept is the gift of living our life reverently. We are assured that Jesus came not that we may have more prayers, or more reading of the Scriptures, or more pious devotions, or more of anything, but only "that [we] might have life and have it more abundantly" (John 10:10, NAB).